T0042745

UNLIMITING
MIND

THE RADICALLY EXPERIENTIAL
PSYCHOLOGY OF BUDDHISM

ANDREW OLENDZKI

Wisdom

Wisdom Publications
199 Elm Street
Somerville MA 02144 USA
wisdompubs.org

Library of Congress Cataloging-in-Publication Data
Olendzki, Andrew.
  Unlimiting mind : the radically experiential psychology of Buddhism / Andrew Olendzki.
    p. cm.
  Includes bibliographical references and index.
  ISBN 0-86171-620-5 (pbk. : alk. paper)
  1. Buddhism—Psychology. I. Title.
  BQ4570.P76O44 2010
  294.301'9—dc22   2010007049

        ISBN 978-086171-620-3   ebook ISBN 978-086171-938-9

21 20 19 18 17
6 5 4 3

Cover design by Phil Pascuzzo. Interior design by LC. Set in Weiss 11 pt/ 15 pt.

Wisdom Publications' books are printed on acid-free paper and meet the guidelines for permanence and durability of the Production Guidelines for Book Longevity of the Council on Library Resources.

❀ This book was produced with environmental mindfulness.
For more information, please visit wisdompubs.org/wisdom-environment

Printed in the United States of America.

Please visit fscus.org.

Note: For accessibility and ease of reading, diacritic marks customarily used in Pali terms have been omitted throughout this work. All translations from the Pali are by the author, unless otherwise noted.

TABLE
OF CONTENTS

Introduction   1

1. THE BIGGER PICTURE

What the Buddha Taught   21
An Organic Spirituality   25
The Non-Pursuit of Happiness   29
The Post-Copernican Revolution   33

2. CARING FOR THE WORLD

Caring for Each Other   39
Healing the Wounds of the World   43
War and Peace   47
Removing the Thorn   51
Burning Alive   55

3. CONSTRUCTING REALITY

Mind and Brain   61
This Fathom-Long Carcass   65
Making the Best of It   69
Unreal Imagination Exists   73
In the Blink of an Eye   77

4. THE PRACTICE

One Thing at a Time   83
Here and Now   87
Tug of War   91
Changing Your Mind   95
Calm in the Face of Anger   99

5. UNDERSTANDING THE TEACHINGS

Interconnected . . . Or Not?   105
Interdependence   109
Beyond Proliferation: *Papañca*   113
Disgusted with Dharma?   117

6. SELF AND NON-SELF

Appearance and Reality   123
Keeping Your Balance   127
Self Is a Verb   131
This World Is Not Yours   135
No Essence   139

7. KARMA

Karma in Action   145
Where the Action Is   149
Whose Life Is This, Anyway?   153
Homo Sophiens   157

8. THE EMERGENCE OF MINDFULNESS

An Abhidhamma Perspective   163

Notes   177
Acknowledgments   181
Index   183
About the Author   191

INTRODUCTION

T HE WORLD STANDS at the threshold of a new era—and it is unclear whether we are entering the worst of times or the best of times. It often seems like we may be witnessing the beginning of the end, as the planet fills up with people, the natural resources sustaining us all dwindle, and the wild creatures of the earth face imminent extinction. At other times it feels more hopeful, that perhaps as a species we may be gradually evolving in consciousness. As we collectively become more open minded, more tolerant, more sensitive to diversity and more concerned with human rights, we occasionally get a glimpse of what it might look like if we were able to leave behind the more primitive ways of dealing with one another inherited from our ancestors. Whether we face times of hope or despair, there is little doubt that we will benefit from understanding ourselves and our behaviors better than we currently do. Psychology is therefore a crucial tool, either for helping us cope with growing difficulties, or for helping us create new possibilities. Our psychological self-understanding may even be a pivotal factor in determining which of these two imaginable futures we come to live.

Scarcely more than a century old, the field of psychology has been one of the defining contributions of the twentieth century. Launched with a perhaps naïve assumption that the mind could be observed directly and objectively as one might the contents of a test tube, much of the discipline soon gave up on the murkiness of introspection in favor of the quantifiable results of behaviorism. At the same time, just as progress in the physical sciences came from the growing ability to see what was invisible to the naked eye by the use of microscopes, telescopes, and mathematical models, so too the early psychologists discovered the unconscious and preconscious mind and developed new tools for exploring and interpreting this mysterious territory. As the century progressed, an explosion of different ways to understand human nature and to heal damaged psyches emerged and progressed, each building on the insights of the others. In recent years a whole new dimension has been added by a growing understanding of the chemistry, architecture, and functioning of the brain, augmented greatly by new imaging technologies.

Yet even so, we also find the field of psychology returning to its introspective roots, under increasing influence from an unlikely source—the contemplative practices of meditation. While the Western sciences developed from the interaction of Indo-European and Mediterranean thought, both of which are fundamentally outward facing, meditation has its roots in the inward-looking perspectives of ancient Indus valley culture. In that part of the world we discover images, thousands of years old, of people in yogic postures and with meditative demeanors, and the artifacts unearthed by archeologists seems to be largely unconcerned with the outward manifestations of culture so dominant further west. Correspondingly, in the early religious history of North India, we find ways of thinking that place far greater emphasis upon exploring the inner world of experience than upon communication from or with external deities. And now, the experience gathered from centuries of meditation practices in the ancient East is beginning to have a significant impact upon how we understand and explore the mind in the modern West.

The outward-facing approach to studying the mind is beginning to reach its natural limitations, as researchers acknowledge that the phenomenon we call consciousness can never be entirely explained from an external perspective—and now we want to know what is really going on in that black box between stimulus and response. Brain scans only become interesting when they are correlated with parallel episodes of internal experience. The subjective component, what it *feels like* to be conscious, is an important part of any model of the mind. Psychotherapists have always known this, of course, and rely daily upon the self-reporting of mental states to access the inner world of their clients, but the way this is done is changing under the influence of the meditative arts. We are learning how much a therapist's empathic abilities are improved by her own meditation practice. We are beginning to learn much more about how clients can be taught to relate to their own internal experience in more skillful ways by relaxing the mind, focusing attention, and allowing the flow of thoughts to pass freely through consciousness. But this is only the first wave of the encounter of Buddhist thought with Western psychology. A second wave is coming, and is likely to have an even more significant impact on how we view ourselves.

Traditionally, the practice of meditation is sandwiched between two other contextualizing teachings: teachings on its root in integrity or virtue, and its culmination in wisdom or insight into the way things actually are. In the world of modern science, the price meditation has paid to become seriously considered by the modern psychological community has been separation from these elements of its classical context. We might imagine this to be akin to the way one might harvest a medicinal plant from the Amazon forest and try to extract and synthesize its active ingredient in the laboratory.

At a recent meeting between brain researchers and Buddhists, such as occur from time to time with the participation of the Dalai Lama, a scientist spoke quite frankly about what was of value to him in Buddhism and what was not. He said essentially that he was happy to wire up virtuoso meditators, such as Tibetan monks with extensive meditative training experience, and record the astonishing anomalies between various of their scanner readings compared with the norm of ordinary waking consciousness. The more remarkable the altered states measured, the more the scientist likes it. But he really was not interested, he admitted, in much of the Buddhist theory that went along with it. In particular, he said, he was not interested in hearing about the ethical skills said in traditional Buddhism to be a precondition of meditative practice, nor of the liberating insights the meditative practices are intended to access. Such things are just not quantifiable, and are therefore inappropriate areas of study from the perspective of the classical Western scientist.

This, I believe, is about to change. There is so much more we can learn from this ancient wisdom tradition, both collectively and personally, that can contribute to the improvement of our world.

I'll say a word about moral integrity and the foundations of classical meditation practice before too long, but I'd like to focus attention primarily upon the insights to which meditation is said to lead us. The three core insights of the Buddhist tradition are the facts of impermanence, of suffering, and of non-self. The first of these refers to the truth that all phenomena, without exception, change; the second recognizes that all experience is structurally incapable of yielding lasting satisfaction; and the third points out the awkward truth that we are not quite what we take ourselves to be. To these we might usefully add the associated ideas of the interdependent arising of all phenomena, and the notion of awakening as a radical psychological transformation. I would like to go through each of these basic teachings in turn, suggesting the particular contribution they are already making and are likely to make to the contemporary field of psychology. These ideas point beyond the practice of meditation as a technique, to the understanding gained by such practices.

Meditation is indeed a tool—but a tool is meant to be used to accomplish good work. Let's look beyond meditation toward wisdom—beyond the finger, toward the moon to which it is pointing.

IMPERMANENCE

At first glance the Buddhist insight into impermanence may not seem too remarkable. Surely every tradition recognizes and appreciates change. What is unique to the Buddhist view is the radical extension of change to *all phenomena whatsoever*. We are used to hearing that some things change, or even that most things change, but it is profoundly challenging to hear that all things change. There is no unchanging essence underlying the effervescent bubbling of our minds and bodies; no unmoved mover standing outside the matrix of cause and effect; no fixed point upon which one can find firm footing; no refuge from the relentless onslaught of aging, illness, and death. We can of course conjure up a concept or an idea of such a stable essence but we cannot, says the Buddha, ever discover it in carefully examined lived experience. We cannot even hold the idea of something stable for long in the shifting currents of the mind.

Indeed the mind itself is the most dramatic example of thoroughgoing change. The very tool we use to construct a world of meaning is itself wobbling, so it is no surprise that we build with it a wobbling world. Classical Buddhist thought considers consciousness to arise and pass away moment after moment, each episode of cognition grasping first one object, then another, in a flowing stream of experience. As one text puts it, "Just as a monkey, making its way through the forest or the jungle, grasps a branch; and releasing it, grasps another: So also that which is called mind, or thought, or consciousness arises in one way and ceases in another—day and night!"[1] Moreover, the objects cognized by consciousness, and the organs by means of which the objects are cognized, are themselves "moving and tottering, impermanent, changing, and becoming otherwise."[2]

Mental health professionals are more familiar than most with the inherent instability of consciousness, confronted as they are by this truth on a regular basis in the various difficulties encountered by their patients. Indeed, this is reflected more generally in English vernacular expressions, which traditionally posit that much mental healing has to do with helping a patient "get grounded," "find firm footing," "hold it together," or "get a grip" when a person feels they are "losing hold" of reality or even of sanity. Perhaps this involves stabilizing a particular identity or self-image, or reestablishing the constancy of an object relation, or even cultivating a series of healthy attachments. Buddhist thought and practice is pointing in the other direction, toward befriending change rather than regarding it as an adversary. The new psychology will have more to do with adapting to change and learning to feel at ease with impermanence than with insulating ourselves from it. With every change something is lost, but something also is gained. When something slips from our grasp, it makes room for something else to come within reach.

How many common psychiatric ailments have their roots in fear of change? The anxiety disorders, of course, but perhaps also difficulties relating to adjustment, avoidance, dependence, and separation. And how many conditions are rooted in an attempt to hold on to something safe and familiar against the onslaught of change? The obsessive and compulsive behaviors come to mind in this regard, along with the full range of addictions. In our culture, people are so often led to feel that change is like a vast and threatening ocean whose waves will sweep them away unless they cling tenaciously to some firmament. But in fact by holding fast to the rocks one only gets pounded by the waves; the damage is caused not by change itself, but by the resistance to it. By identifying impermanence as a fundamental *characteristic* of existence itself, rather than a *problem* to be solved, the Buddhists are encouraging us to let go our hold on illusory solidity and learn to swim freely in the sea of change. Instead of mourning what is lost when alteration occurs, we can open to the opportunities each new moment brings.

Meditation is a form of training for this: each moment's experience must be relinquished in order to be mindful of the next.

SUFFERING

The second great insight of the Buddhist tradition is the inevitable unsatisfactoriness of human experience. Often misconstrued as pessimism or even nihilism, the first noble truth—of suffering—does not deny the experience of pleasure, great joy, or happiness. Nor does it suggest that our lives are not meaningful or worthwhile. Rather it indicates a penetrating examination of the mechanisms of pleasure and happiness, and exposes an inherent limitation in the way our mind/body apparatus naturally constructs experience. Recognizing the unsatisfactoriness of our situation is a natural consequence of seeing the radical impermanence of it all.

It is well known that all animals, humans included, are endowed with deep instincts to pursue the pleasing and avoid the painful. In most creatures this seems to serve well as an adaptive device, helping them locate and consume food, find suitable mates with which to perpetuate the species, and to avoid, flee, or destroy anything that threatens. The hedonic treadmill this puts us on, however, is also the source of many difficulties. The problem, of course, is that pleasure is not ultimately sustainable, and pain is not avoidable. In a healthy human life this might be merely disappointing and inconvenient, but at deeper levels of mental dysfunction this can involve cycles of addiction and denial resulting in profound states of suffering.

Conventional strategies for human happiness entail various ways of maximizing pleasure and minimizing pain, and psychologists are often recruited as allies to help people do this more successfully. A steady parade of positive psychologies make their way up and down the self-help bestseller list, and an increasingly creative array of medications reach the market to help defend against discomfort or insulate from pain. But the shortcoming of these approaches is that they treat the symptoms rather than addressing the underlying causes of the predicament—namely, that unsatisfactoriness, like impermanence, is part of the very fabric of experience.

By accepting as a fundamental axiom that suffering is present as an inescapable component of the human condition, Buddhists make way for a higher-level framing and resolution of the problem. They aspire to a state of well-being that can encompass pain, rather than one that depends on the unrealistic suppression or avoidance of pain. Similarly, they strive to experience pleasure without attachment to or dependence upon its perpetuation. This is done by cultivating *equanimity*, which is a way of being present with pleasure without attachment and of being present with pain without resistance. Equanimity embraces both pleasure and pain, and by doing so can bear them both without suffering.

The Buddhist insight into suffering comes from a subtle understanding of the phenomenology of pleasure and pain. Both are a natural aspect of the mind and body, "hard-wired" so to speak, and thus inevitable in every moment of experience. Sometimes the pleasurable or painful nature of states is dramatically evident, as with physical pain or states of ecstasy, but the feeling tone accompanying all experience may also be so subtle as to be imperceptibly one or the other and will manifest as a neutral feeling. But the feeling tone of objects of experience is not the source of suffering. A fact that can be discerned from careful observation of experience is that suffering is a psychological response to feeling, rather than a feeling itself. Suffering consists of the disappointment felt with the passing away of pleasurable experience, or the annoyance and discontent felt in the face of unwanted or unpleasant experience. In short, the suffering is caused by our wanting things to be different than they are—and this is the second noble truth of Buddhist teachings.

Happiness, or a deep sense of well-being, does not consist of the presence of pleasure or the absence of pain—nor does it depend on these. This too is an important component of the new psychology, and is being applied across a wide range of clinical treatment strategies. In Mindfulness-Based Stress Reduction (MBSR) programs in medical settings, for example, a person can learn to feel well and whole even when diagnosed with a serious illness, facing a terminal outcome, or assailed by chronic pain. Similarly, gaining the ability to tolerate exposure to growing levels of discomfort without triggering phobia, panic, or depression is a skill that can be developed through mindfulness practice, as is the ability to experience pleasure without falling into craving, abuse, and addiction.

There is also a certain relief that comes from knowing that indeed not everything can be fixed. The psychological suffering that derives from not getting what one wants, or from having to deal with what one does not want, can be treated by changing your relationship to wanting. If desire is causing suffering, then letting go of that particular desire, rather than trying to fulfill it or suppress it, is a workable strategy. But the existential facts of aging, illness, and death, both for ourselves and for those we love, are not going to be cured by any amount of psychotherapy, denial, positive thinking, or pharmaceuticals.

At its best, psychology can help us make the most of our current lives by appreciating the poignancy of our predicament, instead of trying to help us escape it. Buddhist psychology, on the other hand, and the insights into the nature of the human condition accessed by sustained meditation, hold out the promise of pointing a way to the third noble truth, the radical cessation of suffering. As we will see, this is to be accomplished not by taking away the pain, which is built in to the human condition, but by learning how to neither hold on to it nor push it away.

NON-SELF

Teachings of non-self are perhaps the most challenging of all the Buddhist insights, particularly for those in a profession so deeply organized around the concept of self. For this reason it is also the most misunderstood of the Buddhist teachings.

Teachings of non-self do not mean the self does not exist, for anything given a name created to express an idea does exist, as such. Whether that name actually pertains to anything found in the world of experience, however, is another matter. We all know how useful an *idea* the self can be as a conventional designation of a particular physical body, personal history, or legal entity. It is also useful in describing a series of stages of development in which certain capabilities emerge, one from another, as a person matures and evolves. None of this is contentious, from the Buddhist view. What the Buddhists are challenging is a series of *assumptions* made about the self that are not sustainable by empirical observation.

One assumption challenged is that the self has some sort of privileged ontological status as a substance, an essence, or a spiritual energy that is something other than the manifestations of a person's natural physical and mental processes. *Self* might be a useful word for referring to a person's body, feelings, perceptions, behavioral traits, and consciousness, but it cannot be construed as something underlying or transcending these manifestations. It may be a good designation of a person, in other words, but a person is not something other than how he or she manifests in experience. In classical Western language what the Buddhists are critiquing is the religious notion of the soul, as something sacred and eternal that is other than the mind and body, and the philosophical notion of consciousness as a mental entity, mysteriously non-extended in time and space. Both of these conceptions, they would argue, may be useful and even beautiful ideas, but do not designate anything that can be known or seen directly.

The other basic assumption about the self that is challenged in Buddhist thought is the notion of *agency*. Again, the creation of agent nouns—of the thinker behind the thoughts or of the doer behind the deeds—is merely an exercise of habit and convention. When one looks closely enough at the stream of consciousness accessible through disciplined meditative skills, one can discern an executive function of intention or will, but there is no one to whom this belongs and no one who is wielding it. Thoughts occur, and some of these thoughts are even intentionally chosen from a range of possible thoughts by a selective function of the mind. Actions too, of body, speech, and mind, must necessarily be undertaken every moment, and there are mechanisms within the mind and body to adjudicate which actions are undertaken at any particular moment from a range of competing alternatives. But we go well beyond the data of experience to conclude from this phenomenology that there is a discrete entity identifiable as the self who is somehow "making" all the decisions. In a way this notion is a modernized version of the theory of mind that postulates a homunculus, a kind of person within the person, who takes executive action.

The fact that choices are indeed made does not necessarily mean that there is an entity standing outside the matrix of cause and effect that is the agent of the choosing. Nor does the absence of such an agent necessarily imply that everything is predetermined and volition is entirely illusory. Both free will and determinism, the two horns of philosophy's classical ethical dilemma, are viewed by Buddhists as ultimately untenable. The middle way between them treads a path upon which we are greatly constrained by conditions and conditioning, but have the ability to create some space, commensurate with our ability to bring mindful attention to the process, in which true choices can be made from a range of possible responses.

All this is now being demonstrated decisively by neuroscientists who increasingly find nothing that maps as a soul in the body or an agent in the mind. We find ourselves now about where the physicists stood a hundred years ago, as they faced the baffling new relativity and indeterminacy of reality with a toolbox filled with theories and images from the era of the "billiard ball universe." The self of popular conception is a comfortable relic of the nineteenth century, hardly suited to cope with the startling revelations of twenty-first century science. Yet psychology is increasingly called upon to account for the textures of lived experience and heal the wounds inflicted when conventional ways of understanding ourselves shatter. Perhaps *non-self*, then, is the radical new perspective that will help enable this to happen.

All the new mindfulness- and acceptance-influenced psychological approaches share the tendency to steer away from stabilized notions of the self, while directing attention instead to the shifting, self-less phenomenology of experience. The level of cognitive macro-construction—where ideas of self and other, success and failure, worth and worthlessness all occur—is a minefield of triggers and snares. Below this threshold—where thoughts and feelings and emotions flow in and out of the mind without definition and without a chance to become established—a person can find some freedom to *not be* the one who suffers.

So: There is indeed a self, but this self is as impermanent, constructed, and dependent upon changing conditions as everything else. If one clings desperately to a particular definition of oneself, as so many of those with psychological disorders tend to do, then one is sure to suffer difficulties. To lose something you are deeply attached to would cause distress for anybody. But if instead one can learn to be non-attached to a particular notion of oneself, and become able to open to new iterations of oneself, new possibilities of becoming a different person in various ways, then the lack of rigid self-identification is more a blessing than a curse. The person who was traumatized in the past need not be the same person who may be free of the impact of that trauma in the future. There may well be a person here now who feels unworthy or unloved, incapable of happiness, but that same person may be nowhere to be seen even a few moments from now. The person deeply caught in cycles of addiction today may be just a character in a story told by a healthier person tomorrow.

The profound plasticity of self, if it can be seen for oneself in the moment-to-moment flow of experience, can be a spectacularly liberating experience.

INTERDEPENDENT ORIGINATION

The Buddhist doctrine of interdependent origination is turning out to be ever more compelling, aligned as it seems to be with emerging trends in systems thinking, chaos theory, and the new physics generally. This teaching basically states that all phenomena arise and pass away in complex patterns of open causality, with no single point or primary material standing in a position of ontological preeminence. A small, closed system, like a chess game or a billiard table, has so few variables that there are a finite number of options and thus all its activity is constrained to a narrow and predictable range. The scale and complexity of natural systems, however, such as the planet's ecosystem or the human brain, allows for a cooperative and distributive approach to causality that can routinely surprise us with its indeterminacy and apparent creativity. However interesting this might be to physicists, it is of particular value to psychologists.

Closely aligned with the insights into impermanence, suffering, and nonself, this teaching describes the human mind and body as a mutual and interdependent arising of phenomena that stand in causal relation to one another, both in any particular moment and over a series of moments unfolding in what is regarded as the stream of consciousness. It is not just that the mind depends upon the body, but the body also depends upon the mind, and both co-arise, co-create, and co-define one another. Furthermore, at the level of carefully examined lived experience, it might not be very useful to make a distinction between the two. The same can be said for perception and feeling, each shaping and informing one another at the very instant of their emergence in experience. So too does intention shape the actions of body, speech, and mind, which also shape the dispositions of our personality and character, but our character then goes on to shape the very decisions and choices that influence how it will unfold in each ensuing moment. In short, that entity we take naïvely to be a person is actually a swirling confluence of mental and physical factors all arising together in concert, mutually conditioning one another for an indescribably brief moment of interaction, and then passing away together to make room for the next moment's configuration.

The good news in all this is that the patterns of causality that shape our experience of reality can be known and understood. Having accepted the changeability of the process by gaining insight into impermanence, having acquiesced to the limitations of gratification inherent in it by acquiring insight into suffering, and having further gone on to glimpse the impersonal nature of it all by achieving insight into non-self, we are now in a position to understand the connections and relationships that weave our reality into what it appears to be. Insight into interdependent origination is not just seeing *that* it is all interrelated, but seeing *how* it is interrelated.

There are certain factors, according to classical Buddhist thought, that always arise together, such as mind and body, or perception and feeling, or craving and ignorance. And there are other things that *never* occur at precisely the same moment (although they may alternate with one another in such rapid succession as to appear to arise together), such as wholesome and an unwholesome thoughts, wisdom and delusion, or mindfulness and attachment. There are some things that naturally lead from one to another, such as desire leading to grasping, intentions leading to dispositions, or tranquility leading to concentration. And there are certain things that, when made to cease, will lead to other things stopping altogether: with the cessation of craving, grasping stops; from the stopping of grasping, the construction of a false sense of self no longer occurs; and when one does not construct in any given moment the view of a self as the central organizing principle of all activities, then the engine of suffering can be brought to a halt. Understanding these relationships can guide our meditation and our psychological understanding, our practices and treatments. When we know how events and the concoctions we make of them are related to one another, we can use that knowledge to disassemble our virtual world and put it back together in a different configuration.

As an example of interdependent origination making a specific contribution to the new psychologies, we can look more closely at the relationship between feeling and desire. As we have seen already, Buddhist psychology regards feeling—the affect tone of pleasure or displeasure—as an intrinsic feature of the mind/body organism. Every moment's experience of an object will come with a feeling tone, whether or not this feeling is accessed by conscious awareness. In response to a feeling of pleasure or pain, an emotional response or attitude of liking or not liking the object may also arise. Most of us conflate these two experiences much of the time, concluding that a particular object is liked or disliked.

However, in fact the object is merely *experienced*, and the liking or disliking of it is something added by our psychological response to it. This difference is a subtle but important nuance. It is the difference between "That is a threatening person" on the one hand and "I feel threatened when I think of that person" on the other. It is the difference between "I am an unworthy person" and "I am a person who is feeling unworthy just now." It is the difference between "I have to be like this because this is the way I am," on the one hand, and "I am like this because of these conditions, and if I manage to change the conditions slightly I am capable of being different in some important ways."

These are all distinctions that contribute greatly to the mindfulness-based psychologies emerging around us, each of which lays great emphasis on the difference between identifying with experience and regarding experience from a position of equanimity and observation.

AWAKENING

One of the criticisms often leveled at modern psychology is its tendency to focus on pathology rather than on health. This is changing, with the growing interest in positive psychologies in general, and with a new focus on happiness in particular. Here again I think Buddhism has something useful to contribute. Despite the elaborate mythological symbolism that has come, over the centuries, to surround it, the Buddha's own description of his awakening—the attainment of nirvana in this very life—is essentially a description of a psychological transformation. Here is a verse attributed to the historical Buddha soon after his awakening that portrays his attainment:

> Indeed the sage who's fully quenched
> Rests at ease in every way;
> No sense desire adheres to him
> Whose fires have cooled, deprived of fuel.
> All attachments have been severed,
> The heart's been led away from pain;
> Tranquil, he rests with utmost ease,
> The mind has found its way to peace.[3]

Notice how the language and imagery of these lines all point to a state of profound well-being, here and now, accessed through understanding the nature of the mind and its behaviors. The word *nirvana* is used here in its original sense—"extinguished." What are extinguished are the fires of greed, hatred, and delusion. The fires are not blown out or stomped out or smothered, but merely deprived of the fuel that feeds them. With the mechanisms for wanting this or not wanting that pacified, the sage rests at ease in every way. This language is reiterated throughout the verse with the use of the words *tranquility, rest, ease,* and *peace.* It is not that sense desires never arise, but that they do not adhere—they do not drive a person to grasp after what is unattainable or harmful. It is not that the attachments needed for healthy development are never made, but that they are severed at the appropriate time to allow for growth beyond what Freud has famously called ordinary human unhappiness. And it is not that there is anything wrong with the heart and the mind themselves, just that they are gently led by understanding away from pain and toward an abiding experience of peace.

Having identified that suffering is caused by a thorn—craving—lodged deep in the heart, the Buddha offered to pull out that thorn, allowing a person to find peace in any circumstance. It turns out that extracting the thorn is not something magical, requiring the special grace or powers of a transcendent being; rather it is something that can be learned by almost anyone. Since the causes of human suffering are ultimately psychological, the healing process is also psychological. This somehow puts the whole enterprise within reach, and renders it attainable.

What is required of our generation is that the causes of human suffering are studied and come to be understood, with whatever tools and disciplines are at our disposal. This is the work of theoretical psychology, and it is greatly assisted in our era by sophisticated techniques of research, experimentation, and collaboration. The wisdom of the Buddhist tradition is one of the tools available, and has something valuable to contribute. In addition, this psychological knowledge needs to be put to work in practical ways to help people. And thus the psychologist is ultimately a healer, and her skill comes largely from knowing how to apply her knowledge in ways that will be transformative and make a difference. All forms of healing require a broad understanding of human nature, the development of effective empathic abilities, and a profound compassion for the well-being of another. Here too the meditative traditions have much to offer, and can be drawn upon as from a deep well. They offer not only training in mindfulness and concentration, but also in loving kindness, compassion, and empathic joy.

INTEGRITY

Let me just add a word about the place of morality or integrity in all this. In the classical Buddhist tradition a profound understanding of the insights outlined here are said to be only accessible through meditation, the skillful development of mindfulness and concentration. And the tradition also holds that such meditative acumen can only emerge from a wholesome ethical context. The reasons for this are not merely cultural, but are rooted in the very nature of consciousness itself.

As one looks closely at the textures of the stream of consciousness, it soon becomes apparent that one's ability to see clearly is directly affected by the moral tenor of the mind. If the mind is regarding the objects of awareness with a degree of attachment, or desire for gratification, for example, its capacity for clarity is diminished. The same is true if any aversion or ill-will manifests. When one either subtly likes or doesn't like, wants or doesn't want the object under observation, the quality of empirical observation is significantly diminished. Likewise if the mind is too sluggish or dull, or if it is agitated by restlessness or by remorse over previous unwholesome behavior, it will be incapable of developing the tranquil alertness needed for insight into the nature of phenomena. Doubts and misgiving will also interfere with the effectiveness of concentration and hinder its deepening.

As with all scientific empirical observation, objectivity is important. Unlike a telescope or a microscope, however, the tool we are using to observe the phenomena at hand—direct, personal, mindful awareness—can be obscured by the slightest tremor of emotional bias or subjective identification. Like the lenses of these instruments, consciousness performs the simple function of bringing an object into view; and like such lenses its ability to do so well is greatly hampered by glare, debris, instability, gloom, or a lack of focus. The hindrances just mentioned have such a limiting effect on consciousness, as do all the unwholesome emotions that give rise to lapses in integrity.

We learn in meditation by trial and error an important fact: the quality of consciousness as a tool for observing itself is profoundly influenced by the moral caliber of its co-arising mental factors.

The natural integrity of consciousness is, I think, very good news for all of us—both as individuals and collectively. What it means for personal development is that one naturally evolves in morality as one progresses in understanding. As we practice meditation and slowly learn to see ourselves more clearly, we also gain an intuitive ability to discern the difference in experience between a wholesome or unwholesome thought, or word, or deed. Advances in integrity, meditation, and understanding all proceed together in a way that gradually guides our path away from suffering and toward the extinguishing of afflictive emotions.

This process of gradual transformation can just as effectively take place on a collective—even a global—level. As we, through our own efforts, alongside so many like-minded people the world over, explore and expand the practice of developing awareness through meditation, introspection, and psychological healing, we contribute incrementally to the clarification of consciousness everywhere. Mindfulness is an instrument for accessing all the cutting-edge insights I have outlined here, and it is also a mechanism for evolving as a species. We as humans are embedded with very primitive instincts for selfishness and for harming one another—but we are also equipped with altruistic impulses to love, protect, and nurture one another. Now we are learning that we also have access to a skill that can be trained and developed, for gaining the freedom to make wise decisions over what aspects of our nature we will enhance and what aspects we will allow to atrophy.

Inquiry into the nature of consciousness, if done directly and experientially, naturally results in a purification of the quality of consciousness. This means that as we come to better understand consciousness, we cannot help but become better people in the process. And it may even be that we can realistically aspire to extinguishing the fires of greed, hatred, and delusion that are ravaging the world we inhabit. This is the work that will decide whether we are entering the worst of times or the best of times.

I for one have confidence that by bringing the healing power of mindful awareness to one affliction at a time, to one person at a time, even to one moment at a time, we stand a chance of eventually turning away from disaster toward a promising new era.

And I trust that after cultivating the practice of mindfulness in your own life, you too will come to share in a portion of this hope for a brighter future.

SECTION 1
THE BIGGER PICTURE

WHAT THE BUDDHA TAUGHT

CONSIDER A TREE: We can look at a tree in terms of its biology or chemistry, its shape, species, or color, or the evocative beauty of its shimmering leaves in the autumn twilight breeze. It's a home to the squirrels, a threat to the foundation of a nearby home, a dinner platter for a host of insects and the many birds that feed on them. It's one thing to the carpenter or boat builder, another to the developer with a site plan, and something else entirely to the ten-year-old boy with some old boards and a handful of nails. It's all a matter of how you look at it.

The same is very much the case for our understanding of what the Buddha taught. Just as the scientist might feel that he or she has a more definitive, "objective" perspective on the tree, so also the scholar of religion tends to wield a certain authority on the teachings of the Buddha—at least in his or her own mind! Even with a sophisticated grasp of hermeneutical issues, an expansive appreciation of the historical context, and a near mastery of ancient linguistic nuance, there is no escaping the pivotal insight of the postmodern world: all meaning is locally constructed. All constructions of knowledge are, in the end, merely constructions.

An understanding of what the Buddha taught is spread across everyone who has ever heard and construed those teachings, because each instance of such an understanding is a local event taking place in a specific moment of interpretation by a particular individual. That individual may be trained in the study of religion, or steeped in the meditative arts, or embedded in a political or religious agenda, or inept at thinking outside a limited comfort zone, or all of the above and more. In fact, the only thing certain is that *everyone* trying to understand what the Buddha taught will be coming at the question from a specific and limited perspective. As such, none of these perspectives stands much chance of getting to what the Buddha "really" taught.

This is not to merely say that "everything is relative" and it is therefore not worth striving for accuracy and nuance in our attempts to understand. How each one of us constructs our local world of meaning is in fact a matter of ultimate concern. Indeed, in a way there is nothing more important or deserving of care. When we construct ourselves and our world in a deluded way, much suffering ensues; but if our local construction of meaning is imbued with wisdom, then we can be largely free of creating this suffering. What guidelines did the Buddha leave for helping us get it right?

To begin with, he seems well aware of the problem. Even during his lifetime, people were regularly misinterpreting his teaching, either inadvertently or deliberately to serve an agenda. "Misguided man, to whom have you ever known me to teach the Dharma in that way?" the Buddha says to Arittha, the former vulture-killer who tries to say obstructions are not really obstructions,[4] and to Sati, the former fisherman who thinks his consciousness will survive his death.[5] From the earliest times he seems to have been regularly misrepresented by those "who declare as spoken or uttered by the Tathagata [the Buddha] what has not been spoken or uttered by the Tathagata."[6]

The Buddha was therefore quite careful about how his teachings were to be handed down, stating, "Two things incline to establishing the non-confusion and non-disappearance of true Dharma: correctly laying down the words and phrases, and correctly interpreting their meaning."[7] And we are told, whenever in doubt about whether a teacher is accurately conveying the teachings of the Buddha, "their words and phrases should be carefully studied and compared with the suttas, and reviewed in the light of the practice."[8]

The first part of this advice is a matter of historical accuracy, critical scholarship, and a certain degree of common sense. But the second part, dealing with "correctly interpreting the meaning" and "reviewing in the light of the practice" is another matter entirely, and calls for a different set of skills.

The Dharma is meant to be *enacted;* it's meant to be lived. It is a blueprint for how to reorganize the mind and body in the present moment, and as such its meaning can only be recovered if it is put to use. The best answer to the question of what the Buddha taught, therefore, will be found not in the texts but in our own experience. It is important to direct attention in *a particular way* within experience, and the instructions for how to do that are indeed to be found in the texts. But the *meaning* of the Buddha's teaching will only manifest when his wisdom is enacted locally, in the transformation of a person.

As he famously tells a group of villagers known as the Kalamas, who are confused by the apparent contradictions of various teachings they have heard, "When you know for yourselves that these things are wholesome . . . these things, when entered upon and undertaken, incline toward welfare and happiness—then, Kalamas, having come to them you should stay with them."[9]

The best way to discern what the Buddha taught is to become what the Buddha taught. Carefully build the raft, diligently paddle it across the river of suffering to the other shore—and become for yourself one who truly knows.

AN ORGANIC
SPIRITUALITY

W E ARE ACCUSTOMED in the West to think of spiritual matters as having to do with placing ourselves in relationship with something somehow greater than ourselves, something "other," and something "out there." At best it is something beautiful, wise, and willing to love us unconditionally. At worst it is powerful, fearful, and capable of judging us harshly or harming us deeply. Some come to know of it through texts of revelation, the teaching of prophets, or the edifices of tradition built upon these foundations. Others intuit it in nature, perceive it in states of non-ordinary experience, or learn of it from wise and trusted elders. In its numerous diverse shapes and forms, this model of the "sacred other" forms the dominant religious paradigm for the Western world.

In ancient India, along the Indus and Ganges river systems, a very different approach to spirituality was discovered and practiced. This system had to do with turning inward rather than outward, with understanding and purifying oneself rather than cultivating a relationship with an Other, and with meditation and asceticism rather than with prayer and ritual. Remnants of this alternative, more organic, approach to spirituality, which grows from lived experience rather than being imported from beyond this world, can still be found in the Yogic, Jain, Buddhist, and Hindu traditions, but they lie for the most part hidden under layers of both ancient and modern Western influence.

Indeed, at least a thousand years before Alexander's fourth century BCE invasion of India, the mantle of Western religiosity was cast over the North

Indian landscape. Aryan migration over the Khyber Pass and settlement of the river valleys in the second millennium BCE displaced the indigenous culture and imposed upon the region a tradition involving hereditary priests, sacred revealed truth, and costly ritual communication with masculine sky gods. Amid this, the more introspective local traditions went underground and to the fringes of the Vedic world, from where they erupted into the mainstream culture from time to time over the ensuing centuries. One such emergence of the older way of thinking occurred when the Upanishads, steeped in the yogic influence of its forest practitioners, were admitted into the Brahmanical fold as an acceptable innovation of the Indo-European Vedic tradition. The ensuing Hinduism was thus at its heart a blending of imported Western and indigenous Indic components.

A more significant incursion occurred when the Buddha started to proclaim his Dharma. From the depths of his personal understanding, gained by arduous ascetic meditation in the wilderness and the radical purification of his mind, the Buddha's teaching burst onto the scene and challenged the Vedic orthodoxy to the core. By the time of the great Buddhist King Ashoka in the third century BCE it looked capable of supplanting the Brahmanical tradition entirely, but with the collapse of Ashoka's empire and the turmoil of recurring waves of invasion, Hinduism was gradually able to regain its dominant position on the Indian spiritual landscape. Buddhism was not only marginalized, but was slowly recast more in line with the previously dominant religious paradigm, and absorbed into the mainstream. Buddha is today seen in India as an incarnation of Vishnu, sent to earth to teach good Hindus to cease animal sacrifice and to become vegetarians. Even today Buddhist teachings are often cast in a terminology originally Hindu: primordial perfection, non-dual awareness, inherently awakened inner nature.

So what are the key features of this more ancient, more organic spirituality taught by the Buddha in his lifetime? To begin with, it is radically experiential. What do you see and feel and touch and know, *for yourself*, when you attend to the immediacy of the present moment with steady and focused awareness? Knowledge coming from without is fraught with illusion, projected from the mysterious depths of the psyche. According to the sages of the river valleys, only by exploring the inner landscape, the nuances and subtle textures of lived experience, can useful and authentic wisdom be discovered.

Fearless and honest introspection will soon reveal the basic flaws of the human condition; this is the noble truth of suffering. The mind and body are riddled with stumbling blocks, choke points, nodes of tension, knots of pain, and a veritable fountainhead of selfish, hurtful, and deluded psychological stuff. The mind's capacity for awareness, the "knowing" that arises and passes away, drop by drop in the stream of consciousness, is constantly hindered, fettered, intoxicated, and obscured by such internal defilements. The enterprise of organic spirituality is to untangle this jumble, to untie these knots, to unbind the mind—moment by moment, breath by breath—from the imprisoning net of unwholesome and unhealthy manifestations. The reward for a life of careful inner cultivation is the liberation of the mind through wisdom—a remarkable transformation of the mind that awakens it to its full potential of awareness without obstruction or limitation.

Volumes could be written about the details of this science of liberation, about its discoveries of impermanence, selflessness, and suffering, its analysis of the psychophysical organism into sense spheres, aggregates, and elements, the subtle workings of interdependent origination and cessation, or about the remarkable territory mapped out by the exploration of inner states. But the pivotal discovery of this ancient spirituality is that the world of human experience is a "virtual" world, constructed each moment by every individual mind and body to patterns of human invention and instinct.

Mind and body are natural expressions of a natural world. Their suffering is natural; their liberation from suffering is natural. The "sacred other" is as much a construction as are notions of "permanence," "selfhood," and "beauty." It's not that such things "don't exist" or cannot be the source of considerable meaningfulness. It's just that they are not "out there" in the ways the Indo-European religious reflex takes for granted. Rather, they are projected by the same inner mechanism that orders all other human constructions, the workings of desire.

It's not surprising that this radical alternative to the dominant paradigm was misunderstood by the Buddha's Brahmanical contemporaries, misrepresented for centuries by their ancestors, and continues to be over-looked by modern heirs of the Indo-European spiritual tradition.

Yet it continues to beckon, quietly offering its compelling perspective on the human condition to those willing to look inward rather than outward and upward.

THE NON-PURSUIT
OF HAPPINESS

HERE ARE two fundamentally different approaches to the attainment of happiness. One is so deeply embedded in our civilization almost everything in our culture supports it; the other is a radically different view offered by the Buddha twenty-five centuries ago. Which approach is likely to contribute most to our own happiness? My bets are on the Buddha.

We should begin by offering a rudimentary definition of happiness, for which we might fruitfully turn to modern systems theory. Every organism, by which we mean a functioning system of any kind nestled within other systems (ecological, biological, social, psychological, political, etc.) has some sort of membrane or way of defining a boundary between internal and external, between the organism and its environment. A system's health or well-being, which at the human scale we call happiness, might be simply defined as a state of equilibrium between inner and outer states. For example, an amoeba whose internal temperature matches that of its surrounding water might be called healthy, and if we are willing to anthropomorphize a bit, we might even call it happy. But if the water it wriggles in suddenly plummets in temperature, then there is a mismatch between the conditions in which the amoeba is comfortable and those it is currently experiencing. In human terms such an uncomfortable tension is called unhappiness, which manifests as a yearning for the disequilibrium to be resolved—desire.

Which brings us to the two strategies for achieving happiness: One is to change the external environment to meet the needs (or wants) of the organism; the other is to change the internal state of the organism to adapt itself to the environment. We can either change the world to satisfy our desires, or change our desires by adapting to the world. Both strategies aim at removing the agitation of desires, one by fulfilling them and the other by relinquishing them.

The human psychophysical organism is structured in such a way that the gratification of desire usually means getting each of the six senses to experience its object in conjunction with a feeling tone of pleasure. Of course we all know that such moments cannot be sustained; but that does not seem to be a major deterrent. Even if we know that we cannot satisfy all of the senses all of the time, the satisfaction of some of the senses some of the time is still taken to be the appropriate thing to do with ourselves on this earth. Virtually everything in our culture reinforces this, and we are continually encouraged to define ourselves by the range of our desires and our success at gratifying them.

The compulsion to change the world to calm our desires is ultimately based on an idea of how things should be, and as such is dependent upon the degree of wisdom we can bring to bear at any moment. We might expound a number of altruistic ideals to change the world for the better, yet even when we are making progress in some ways, we can be causing major problems in others. It is not that some desires are not more worthy than others; the problem is with the nature of desire itself.

Because we are so imbued with the notion that happiness is something to be pursued by the continual transformation of the external, it can sound odd to hear the Buddha talk of uncovering happiness within. He acknowledged the inevitable presence of disequilibrium, which he called *dukkha* or suffering, but suggested we seek out its internal causes, understand them, and solve the problem by means of internal adjustments. According to the Buddha's analysis, it is not the objective discrepancy between the internal and the external conditions that is the source of unhappiness; it is the *desire* for the external to change (or to not change, as the case may be), which is itself an internal state. Conditions in the world are notoriously unstable and subject to forces beyond our control, while internal desires are intimate and more accessible. It is simply more efficient to adapt to the world than to alter it.

This is especially true because the mind, as the creator of desires, will inevitably generate more desires than can ever be satisfied by even the most successful series of external changes. Even if we were very good at making everything outside of ourselves be just the way we ourselves want it to be (a ludicrous thought, you must admit), we could fundamentally never get everything perfect: because our desires are always changing, because they are often conflicting, and because the changes of the environment can never keep up with the pace of the wanting mind. The satisfaction of desire as a strategy for happiness will always be a doomed enterprise.

Which brings us to meditation, which involves the continual monitoring of subjective states of mind and body. The full range of sense experience— sights, sounds, odors, flavors, physical sensations, and mental phenomena—manifests as moments of knowing. The material body, feelings of pleasure and pain, perceptions of various sorts, dispositions, activities, and intentions are all known; even knowing itself is known. And through all this experience are woven the threads of desire, the subtle wantings of the mind for things to be like this or like that, not quite like this or not quite like that. Moment after moment one practices letting go of these desires when meditating, surrendering to the world as it is; gently adapting to a moment, and then gently adapting to another moment.

Such inner response to experience reestablishes the equilibrium between ourselves and our world. As each more subtle desire is revealed, we let go of it and rest comfortably in the cessation of that desire. In this way happiness is not *pursued and attained*, but is rather *discovered and uncovered* within. There, underlying the tensions created by wanting, it lies.

The Buddha often talked about the sublimity of happiness that lay beyond the satisfaction of the senses. But this is not the realm in which most of us can live, except, perhaps, for precious moments now and then. What about the push and pull of the busy world, built around the tyranny of desire? How in this context do we live the wisdom of the Buddha's ancient alternative?

The path of transformation laid out by the tradition is a gradual one, a path of gently replacing one set of habits with another. Most of us are too much a product of the world that shaped us to entirely give up our embedded attitudes of changing the world to meet our needs. And, of course, this strategy of personal psychological accommodation does not obviate the need to act skillfully to change things that cause obvious harm or embody great injustices. But I suspect there are far more opportunities to adapt instead of alter than we might at first imagine. And as we get the knack of it, others will present themselves.

Let's try giving the world a rest from our restless need to transform it, and work a bit more on changing ourselves. I trust the Buddha's promise that by doing so we will be happier in the long run.

THE POST-COPERNICAN
REVOLUTION

P EOPLE USED TO naïvely think the earth was at the center of the universe, and that the sun and all the stars revolved around us. Then
Copernicus came along and declared the thoroughly counter-intuitive
truth that, appearances to the contrary, the earth in fact orbited the sun.
This launched a scientific revolution that focused on attempting to study
everything from an objective stance, as if we could hover outside ourselves
and get a disembodied perspective on it all. This way, the objectivist story
goes, our view is not cluttered by all that messy, subjective stuff that only
distorts reality to conform with our personal illusions.

Well, the last few centuries have been a pretty good run for the objective sciences, but the cutting edge of all our postmodern understanding is
putting us right back where we started—at the center of the world. It turns
out that the non-personal "objective" perspective on everything cannot ultimately be sustained except as a sort of thought experiment. We are embedded in the world, whether we like it or not. All views are a view from
somewhere, and we are discovering again and again that where you are
looking from makes a big difference to what you see.

The Buddhists realized this a long time ago. They begin their take on
things from the inside out, so to speak, rather than from the outside in. We
are used to starting with a grand explanation of it all—from the big bang
to coagulating stardust to roiling primordial soup to amoebas to digital
watches—and then, almost as an afterthought, trying to figure how we as
individuals fit in to it all. The ancient contemplative traditions of India

started with the empirical phenomenon of consciousness—the capacity we each have for awareness—and developed a model of existence flowing out from that. The view around which they built their understanding is one becoming more familiar to the contemporary cognitive and neurosciences, namely that each individual mind and body system constructs meaning as a synthetic momentary act. Each one of us, in other words, is planted squarely in the center of a virtual world we create for ourselves every moment.

The implications of this are remarkable, but let's first dispatch a few mistaken ideas about what this might mean. It does not imply the solipsistic idealism that nothing exists outside myself, or that my mind is creating all the physical universe at my whim. Nor does it mean that I have a lot of power to control things, or even that I am the most important thing there is. It also does not mean that other people don't matter, or that my pursuit of pleasure and avoidance of pain is the primary purpose of the universe. One might be forgiven for thinking so from time to time, but none of these views are conducive to sustainable well-being. At the same time, we need to be careful not to draw mistaken conclusions in the other direction: My life is not necessarily absurd, pointless, or without intrinsic value. It need not be the case that without reference to a transcendent reality greater than myself, for example, or without an agenda created by others, my life has no meaning.

The implication of being at the center of our world, in the Buddha's estimation, is that we have both the freedom and the responsibility to influence how it all unfolds. The pivot point around which the world of our experience turns is the node of conscious awareness manifesting in this particular body at this particular moment. An episode of consciousness arises again and again, like the firing of a spark plug, and interacts with sense objects and sense organs, perceptions, feelings, and attitudes, to shape a glimpse of a meaningful order. With innumerable glimpses strung together in a stream of consciousness, the view of a coherent narrative unfolds.

The mechanics of this process are mostly hard-wired, thank goodness, but we have direct access to the very best part of it: we have the privilege of paying attention to all that is happening, and for it to be illuminated with mindful awareness. Being at the center of the world, we have pretty good seats for the show. It's all flowing around us and through us; it's all happening for us and by means of us. And when we decide to participate, by deliberately and wholeheartedly attending to the details of arising and passing phenomena, it can become a transcendent experience. Regarded objectively, this individual fountain of consciousness might not seem like such a big deal, compared to the other splendors of the universe, but when entered into subjectively, with direct awareness, it can become the most splendid of all things.

The Buddha invites us to move beyond the limitations that come from allowing ourselves to be defined by external conditions, a lump of earth orbiting some other sun, and to embrace the central source of our existence. By opening our awareness to what is pouring out of us each moment, and moreover by intentionally shaping what unfolds in wholesome and altruistic ways, there are few limits on how bright we can become—right here and right now.

SECTION 2
CARING FOR THE WORLD

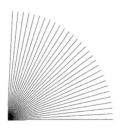

CARING FOR
EACH OTHER

ONE TIME when the Buddha was walking among the dwellings of
his monks, he came across a monk who was very ill with dysentery,
lying alone in his own excrement. He asked the monk why none
of the others were caring for him and was told that he was of no use to the
other monks, so they left him to cope with his illness alone. The Buddha
immediately sent his attendant Ananda for a bowl of water, and together
they washed the sick monk and raised him onto a bed. He called together
all the monks of the community and asked why this monk was left unattended in his distress. He was given the same answer: "He is of no use to
us, Lord."[10]

"You monks no longer have a mother or father to care for you," he said
to them. "If you do not care for one another, who else will care for you?" He
used the occasion to lay down one of the principles guiding the monastic
community, enjoining the monks to care for each other in times of illness.
It is a poignant story, revealing a side to the Buddha seldom seen in the
Pali texts. More importantly, I think it has something to say to us about the
situation we all find ourselves in today, and can offer inspiration and guidance on how we can best get ourselves out of difficulty.

Surely one of the main problems we face, as a species and as a planet, is
that we are in some sense collectively lying in our own excrement—all the
waste products produced by our consumption, from garbage and debris to
chemical toxins and exotic poisons, are oozing out of us and soiling the
environment we inhabit. And what the Buddha says about everything else

surely applies here: Nothing happens without a cause. Things are the way they are, not because of chance or the will of a deity, but because people have acted in particular ways and generated particular consequences. The world we inhabit is the product of our own actions, which are themselves direct reflections of our minds.

We may also, like the early Buddhist community, be on our own. The Buddha has suggested that we too, in a larger sense, are without a mother and father to take care of things for us. Mother Earth, once thought to be all-forgiving and capable of absorbing any abuse we could heap upon her, is not the infinitely benevolent resource we thought she was and can be damaged by our mistreatment. And our Father who is in heaven, though perhaps (in the Buddhist view) immensely old and lord over a host of devas, is nevertheless subject to the laws of karma, will eventually cycle out of his place at the top of the world system, and is not sufficiently omnipotent to make it all work out for us in the end.

If we do not care for one another, who else will care for us? Who among us has the right to say of another, "He is of no use?" For better or worse, whether we like it or not, we are all in this together. Learning how to care for one another is a central part of the path and of the practice.

As the Buddha laid down the monastic injunction for the monks to care for each other, he placed the responsibility first upon the ill monk's preceptor, then upon his teacher, and finally upon all his companions. Transposing this to our collective secular situation, we might say that we look first to our elected officials, as the dominant authority in our society, to take responsibility for helping clean up our mess and healing ourselves, but if these prove inadequate then it is up to the many other people in positions of influence to take the lead and show the way. If these too cannot manage to do so, then it is up to each and every individual to step up and personally lend a hand. There is no one else to whom the duty can be passed.

The filth of dysentery is washed away with clear water. The toxins of greed, hatred, and delusion oozing from the human psyche are cleansed with generosity, kindness, and wisdom. Once we've been lifted from the dirt onto a place of greater purity and dignity, we can begin the gradual process of healing itself. The Buddha, in his role as physician, has laid out in the

Four Noble Truths a protocol for recovery: Identify the symptoms, understand their causes, use this knowledge to counteract and remove the causes, and then diligently follow a detailed regimen for effecting the cure.

But the medicine can only heal us if we take it. What if we administer the medicine of the Dharma to one another, each lifting the other up and showing compassion for one another's suffering? Even to those we do not particularly like or understand; even to those who are "of no use" to us; even, dare I say, with our own hand?

HEALING THE WOUNDS
OF THE WORLD

MANY OF US TODAY are thinking about security, wondering how best to keep our families and our nations safe. Because so much of the danger in the world lately seems to be focused in the Middle East and southwest Asia, we most often encounter Islamic, Jewish, and Christian perspectives on affairs in these regions. Perhaps it would be helpful to hear from one of the other great world religions. What is the Buddhist view of how to achieve safety and security in the world's trouble spots, and how might this outlook apply closer to home in our own communities?

One thing the Buddhist tradition emphasizes is the interdependence of all things. The world we inhabit is a vast network of interrelated systems—natural systems of earth, air, fire, and water, living systems of plants and animals, and human social, political, and economic systems. In such a world every action has far-ranging effects, and often influences things in ways that go well beyond what is immediately apparent. This is particularly true of acts of violence, which often do as much or more harm to the perpetrator or to innocent bystanders as to the intended victim.

One morning while walking barefoot in ancient India the Buddha came across a young man who was pouring oblations and uttering mantras of protection while facing in each of the six cardinal directions (including nadir and zenith). "How can you think such things will bring you security?" the Buddha asked the youth. "I learned this from my father," came the reply. "It is how things have always been done." "Listen," said the

Buddha, "and I will tell you how to make sure that each of the directions is truly safe and free from danger."

The Buddha went on to describe how real security comes from cultivating and nurturing the network of social relationships within which each person finds themselves embedded.[11] Caring for, supporting, and respecting one's parents as though they were the eastern direction will ensure that they in turn will care for, support, and respect their children. Doing the same for one's wife or husband as the west, teachers and supervisors as the south, friends and colleagues as the north, workers and subordinates as the nadir, and spiritual guides as the zenith will similarly result in a reciprocal response and the strengthening of the social bonds that connect one's whole community.

For example, being kind, generous, and honest with your spouse is the best protection from the turmoil of divorce and acrimony. Treating your employees fairly and sharing the fruits of their labor equitably is the best way to encourage their loyalty and cooperation. Nurturing your own children with love and devotion is more likely to result in them caring for you when you are eventually in need.

But what about those who would wish us ill? How does this basic principle apply to our country in the context of response to, for instance, terrorist attack? Our deeper, more lasting security will only come from the gradual transformation of our relationships with people who are currently considered adversaries and who presently would do us harm. Turning enemies into friends is a surer way of protecting ourselves than returning violence with more violence.

History records a kaleidoscopic swirl of changing relationships between people, tribes, cultures, and nations. We can focus on all the outbreaks of hostility, just as we can always conjure a reason to launch new hostilities. But every one of the conflicts of the past has eventually healed, just as every fight taking place today will someday be a historical remnant. Not too long ago America felt under tremendous threat from the Soviet Union, while today we refer to Russia and most of its former satellites as friends or even allies. Our new-found security has not come from our nuclear stockpile, but from the transformation of our relationship with a former adversary. From a Buddhist perspective, just as there are no essential selves outside a unique set of shaping conditions, there are no struggles, conflicts, or rival-ries outside of the particular historical circumstances shaping an era. In this view, there are no enemies, only countries with which the process of rec-onciliation has not yet been completed.

Sometimes the conditions needed to allow for reconciliation involve a change of regime or some other dramatic change. But change is inevitable, and in most cases the changes leading to healing will happen by natural evolution. To do so by violent means amounts to war and, once loosed, the dogs of war tend to wreak havoc in unimaginable ways. Instead of sooth-ing an area of conflict by trying to heal the ruptured relationship, we are inflicting a fresh wound, with its own set of new and expanding dangers. And this simply does not make us safer; rather it exposes us to greater and often unforeseen hazards.

A country will be safe from terrorism when its relationships with all par-ties in all directions are honest, noble, and just. As the Buddha tells the brahmin youth, security comes from aligning our attitudes and policies with the behaviors that will bring out the best in others, rather than doing the very things that are sure to provoke or entrench them. It is a principle that works at every scale: Healing through the cultivation of change in relationship can occur with ancient adversaries, with the developing nations of the world, with the population that swells our prisons, or with alienated members of our own family.

This is not idealism; it is rooted in a deep understanding of human nature. One trend of our country's leadership has been to pour the oblations and mumble the mantras of the last century—beating the drums of war—and in the long run this will only increase the danger faced by the entire world. Let us try a wiser way.

It requires diligence not only to the north, the south, the east, and the west, but also to the nadir of those less developed than ourselves and to the zenith of our own higher values and aspirations. It is by embodying the principles we hold dear that we can help others rise out of unwholesome intentions to harm us.

And it is only by having no enemies that we can all ultimately be safe and free from fear.

WAR AND PEACE

IRST THE BAD NEWS: the mess we are making of our planet is caused by our own greed, hatred, and delusion. Aside from the existential afflictions of aging, death, and at least some of the illnesses, every instance we see of human misery, injustice, affliction, or pain will, upon sufficient and sometimes even cursory investigation, be shown to be rooted in the attachment, aversion, or ignorance of some person or group of people together. Human beings construct the world of human experience, and when people act, speak, or even think badly we all wind up with an afflicted world.

Now the good news: each of the unwholesome roots of human behavior has an equal and opposite wholesome root. Generosity and renunciation stand as the antithesis of greed; kindness and compassion are at hand as alternatives to hatred; and wisdom is accessible as an antidote to ignorance and delusion. Despite the headlines, the human realm is suffused with countless daily episodes of goodness, and a great deal of what gets created by people each moment is wonderful.

At the heart of the human condition lies the capability to choose between wholesome and unwholesome attitudes. It might often feel like we have no choice, because of layers of behavioral conditioning or the influence of powerful persuasive forces. And it may also be that many of the choices we make are unexamined, unconscious, and thus do not feel like choices at all. But this ability to decide, to deliberately give energy to either wholesome or unwholesome inclinations, to steer a course, if you will, between one option and another, is something precious that distinguishes us from machines or animals.

Which brings us to the matter of war and peace, and the mental states that project them. While outwardly war is characterized by distrust, violence, and a whole lot of killing, these are merely the manifestations of inner states of turmoil, such as fear, anger, hatred, and cruelty. Peace on the other hand is characterized by such outward features as harmony, honesty, mutual respect, and cooperation. The inner states generating these activities include such factors as tranquility, kindness, compassion, and unselfishness. A mind at war is organized around unwholesome qualities, and makes room for the wholesome only briefly and reluctantly. A mind at peace, organized around wholesome states of mind, may still evoke the unwholesome qualities needed from time to time to deal with a threat, but otherwise rests easy.

This, however, is what is at stake: "Whatever a person frequently thinks and ponders upon, that will become the inclination of his mind," said the Buddha.[12] In thinking or acting the way we do, we are shaping ourselves in the process. This means that if we organize around a war footing, we are creating the conditions for further violence, while if we cultivate and manifest a peaceful demeanor we will be setting the stage for more peace.

In war mode, all mental states will be generating unwholesome effects, even those that arise and pass away in between the occasional episodes of necessary unwholesomeness. In peace mode, wholesome effects are produced by default, working wholesome changes upon oneself and the world.

In other words, a peaceful person who must from time to time muster war-like qualities to ensure her survival or to protect the innocent will generate wholesome karma most of the time—except in those brief moments when harder stuff is called for. By contrast, a person geared-up in war mode is producing unwholesome effects beyond what is minimally required by the duty to safeguard one's self and others. Such a person will also experience episodes of peacefulness from time to time, but these will be rare in the context of an ongoing unwholesome intentional stance.

If a person feels threatened, he may hold himself continually on a war footing—suspicious, aggressive, violent—and feel this is what is needed to protect himself. By doing so, however, he may well be provoking from all those he encounters the very behaviors he is trying to deflect. Showing suspicion, aggression, and violence, he invites these very responses from others, and thus he is contributing directly to his own lack of real security. What appears to be an effective short-term strategy turns out to do considerable long-term and unforeseen damage.

If, on the other hand, a person stays for the most part in a peaceful intentional stance, she will regularly influence people in the direction of the wholesome. Even if she must rear up from time to time to face down the evil intentions of others, she is not distorting her peaceful character in the moments intervening between these incidents. While there might be some greater short-term risk, the long-term prospects of a wholesome outcome are much improved.

A useful analogy for this point of view can be found in the science of stress-reduction. Humans are designed to generate intense but brief eruptions of fear (for flight) and aggression (for fight) in response to occasional threats from predators. It is natural for attachment (to survival) and aversion (to becoming a predator's lunch) to be evoked in times of danger, but it is equally natural for these to subside when the danger is passed and for the human mind and body to fall back into the more peaceful default mode of a nurturing, cooperative mammal.

When an unskillful decision interferes with this cycle, such as the decision to place oneself on a sustained war footing, then the mind and body are subjected to significant amounts of long-term, low-grade damage in the form of stress. Such a stance harms oneself internally by generating an unremitting stream of unhealthy karmic factors (such as high blood pressure in an individual or low tolerance for diversity in a society), and it harms oneself externally by provoking others into conflict with us. Perhaps it is time to take the insights gained about the healthy effects of stress reduction in the medical field and apply them to the body politic. Our nation as a whole, I suspect, would gain much from the practices of stress reduction, and from gradually replacing policies rooted in fear with policies rooted in wisdom.

REMOVING THE THORN

Fear is born from arming oneself.
Just see how many people fight!
I'll tell you about the dreadful fear
That caused me to shake all over.
Seeing creatures flopping around,
Like fishes in shallow water,
So hostile to one another!—
Seeing this, I became afraid.[13]

In the remarkable passage above, from the *Attadanda Sutta*, the Buddha speaks frankly of his fear and dismay about the state of society. The image of fishes flopping around in the shallows seems as apt today as ever. As the world's resources diminish and the number of people in need of them increases, things may well get only more desperate. But even in the Buddha's time the situation seemed overwhelming. The Buddha acknowledges his despair, but he also describes his breaking through to a deeper understanding:

Seeing people locked in conflict,
I became completely distraught.
But then I discerned here a thorn—
Hard to see—lodged deep in the heart.
It's only when pierced by this thorn
That one runs in all directions.
So if that thorn is taken out—
One does not run, and settles down.

This pivotal insight shapes how conflict and peace are to be understood in Buddhist tradition. Human society is formed by the collective action of its individuals; it thus reflects the qualities of heart and mind of each person. Peace in people's hearts creates peace in the world; turmoil in people's hearts creates turmoil in the world. The harmful behavior people manifest in the world can be seen as having a single cause. That cause is desire.

Desire comes in two forms: attachment and aversion. The first makes us grab after the things we like and try to hold on to them at all costs. The second makes us avoid or resist the things we don't like and, if possible or necessary, destroy them. Attachment leads us to consume resources at any cost, take from others what has not been given to us, and drives us to exploit others for personal gain. It also underlies such personality traits as pride, arrogance, conceit, selfishness, and the lust for power. Aversion compels us to turn away from what we find unpleasant, to shut out or discriminate against those we don't like, and to destroy what we fear or what we don't understand. It also causes such aberrant behaviors as violence, cruelty, bigotry, and other acts of hatefulness.

But these thorns in the heart can be removed. It is just the thorn, driving us mad with pain and fear, that makes us crazy enough to hurt and hate, that makes us lose touch with our innate goodness. Like a ferocious lion with a thorn in its paw, we are only in need of a healer to come pull out the thorn that afflicts us. The Buddha was such a healer. Having diagnosed the problem as desire—so embedded in the heart that it is often hard to see— his prescription was simply to apply awareness to the problem, and in massive doses. Because the workings of desire are hidden in the unconscious functioning of the mind, we must bring greater consciousness to bear on the moment. We have only to learn to see things clearly, and a natural process of healing will occur.

To heal the individual wounds brought about by desire the Buddha prescribed mindful meditation: the careful, moment-to-moment observation of everything arising and falling in the field of phenomenal experience. When we are able to see what is actually occurring within us, wisdom will gradually and naturally evolve. The principle is simple, but it takes practice and a great deal of perseverance. To heal the collective wounds of our planet, likewise brought about by desire in its various forms, it seems to me we might apply the same prescription. The way to bring collective mindfulness to bear on the collective field of experience is through witnessing and sharing what has been seen by others.

We can see many examples today of the beneficial things that can happen when an atrocity is caught on tape and shared widely with others, or when evidence of wrongdoing is brought to light and exposed before the court of world opinion. Just as the evil we are capable of as individuals lies lurking unexamined deep in our psyches, surging unseen from the darkness to highjack our behavior when inattentive, so also much of the cruelty and abuse that takes place in the world is hidden from view. And just as uncovering our personal demons can begin a process of healing, so also can the revealing of cruelties and injustices that have been kept secret have a transformative effect on global misbehavior.

According to the Buddha, the human world is protected by the "twin guardians," two forces in the mind that watch over and guide moral behavior. The first guardian of the world is *hiri*, a word that connotes conscience, moral intuition, and self-respect. It refers to that within the human psyche which knows the difference between right and wrong, between what is noble and ignoble, between what is worthy of respect and what is not. Each of us has within us an innate moral compass, and it is the view of the Buddhist tradition that religion is not the source of this but rather a form by which it is given expression. The second guardian of the world is *ottappa*, which comprises such notions as social conscience, a cultural or collective sense of morality, and respect for the opinions and the rights of others.

Anything we do that is wholesome will be done with the support and guidance of these two inner guardians. Conversely, everything we do that is unwholesome can only be done when these moral guides are disregarded. So if there is something morally reprehensible occurring in an individual or in a society, it means that we lack sufficient clarity of awareness of what we are doing. It means we are temporarily blinded by our greed, hatred, or delusion, or by some combination of the three, such that we refuse to attend openly to the deeds we are committing. When attention has been brought to bear on the matter—in sufficient amounts, with sufficient intensity, and with sufficient honesty—we will naturally shy away from doing harm to ourselves, to others, and to both.

This may sound unrealistic, but it actually reflects something deeply true about how the mind works. So let's spend more time on that collective meditation cushion, shining the light of awareness into the dark corners of the world. The possibility exists for radical universal transformation.

We have merely to start the process, in our own mind, and the rest will fall naturally into place.

BURNING ALIVE

EVERYTHING IS BURNING!" said the Buddha almost twenty-five centuries ago. "Burning with what? Burning with the fires of greed, hatred and delusion."[14]

These words seem prophetic today, as our planet is slowly warmed by the fires blazing in our furnaces and engines, by the explosion of our bullets and bombs, and by the raging delusions around which our entire world seems to be organized. There is not a single problem we face as human beings, other than tectonic (earthquakes), astronomical (meteor strikes), or existential (aging and death) problems, that does not find its origin in the greed, hatred, or delusion of a person or of institutions made up of persons.

Like a fire, greed is more a process than a thing. It is the act of combusting, the activity of consumption, the process by means of which organic resources are quickly reduced to a heap of ash. And it is by its nature insatiable, since the moment one desire is gratified another inevitably flares up demanding also to be sated. Greed drives an unquenchable compulsion to consume and, as the guiding hand of our economic system, its reach is rapidly becoming global. As it burns it throws off a compelling light, dazzling us with the pleasure of its shapes and colors. We delight in playing with this fire.

Hatred is a hotter, bluer, more sinister fire. It seethes among the coals, preserving its heat over time, until blasting forth suddenly with a surge of the bellows. It can simmer as discontent, smolder as suppressed rage, or lurk hot underground as a molten magma of loathing. When it does flare up the fire of hatred scorches all in its path indiscriminately, often searing the innocent bystander with the ferocity of its angry flames.

Delusion is more subtle. As the lamp behind the projector, the shimmer within the illusion, or the reflection in a mirror, delusion shines with a softer light and illuminates indirectly. Delusion can be lovely, which is half the problem; and light doesn't always shows the truth, which is the other half of the problem. Delusion shows things as other than they are—as stable, satisfying, personal, and alluring. Its optical tricks are endearingly creative, so much so that sometimes we hardly know where the light leaves off and the darkness begins. Delusion leads us to revel in wielding the fires of greed and hatred, oblivious of the harm inflicted both on ourselves and on those around us.

The Buddha identifies these three fires as the origin of both individual and collective suffering. Things do not become the way they are by chance, for no reason, or because a deity makes them so. Indeed, it is the quality of our intention that shapes the world we inhabit, and our world is burning up because of the fires smoldering in our hearts. Resources are becoming depleted because people are greedily consuming them and lusting for the money produced thereby. People are being killed, raped, tortured, and exploited because they are hated, because other people do not regard them as being worthy of respect or equal in rights. And the world blindly, stupidly, deceptively plods along this path to destruction because people do not know—or do not want you to know—any better.

Yet here's the thing: This is *good* news. Why? Because the causes of all the trouble have been exposed, and by knowing them we stand a chance of overcoming them. How much worse if our problems were due solely to, say, continental drift or to an inevitably approaching meteor! What then would be our recourse? Fortunately, fire is actually a very fragile phenomenon. Diminish its heat, starve it of oxygen, or take away its fuel, and it does not last. In fact it is entirely dependent upon external conditions; change any of these conditions, and it will always go out. The Buddha put out the fires of greed, hatred, and delusion in himself, and showed us all how to do the same thing. Perhaps we can use this knowledge to quench the fires that are heating our planet and devouring our world.

Something empowering happens when the issue shifts from external to internal. We have access to ourselves. We have the ability to make internal changes when the mechanisms for change are within our reach. A slight shift of attitude, a minor adjustment of priorities, an occasional opening to a wider perspective, the glimpse of a good greater than the merely personal—these all contribute in a small way to turning down the heat, damping the flames. And since we are faced not with a single enormous fire but with billions of little fires, each one ablaze in one person, miniscule changes in one mind here and one heart there can add up to a dramatic reduction of greenhouse defilements.

All it would take is a gradual increase in generosity and an incremental reduction of the need for gratification to begin to turn down the heat of greed's fire. Planting a tree rather than cutting one down engages a different quality of mind, an attitude of giving rather than of taking. Appreciating when we get what we need, instead of demanding that we get what we want, removes fuel from the fire of discontent instead of stoking it. The flames of hatred are banked when we shoot a picture instead of an animal, when we fight injustice rather than our neighbor, when we include someone different in our circle, or even when we relinquish our hold, ever so slightly, on something that annoys us in a mundane moment of daily life. Just as heat is pumped into the system each moment through inattention, so also can heat be consistently and inexorably extracted as we bring more mindfulness to what we think, feel, and do. A tranquil mind is a cooler mind, and indeed the Buddha has described the movement toward awakening as "becoming cool" (siti-bhuta, in Pali).[15]

The solution to so many of our problems is very close at hand. Look within, reach within, and turn down the thermostat just a degree or two—every moment.

If we do not feed the fires, they will surely go out. For they are ultimately unsustainable.

SECTION 3
CONSTRUCTING REALITY

MIND AND BRAIN

From the unseen, states come and go,
Glimpsed only as they're passing by;
Like lightning flashing in the sky—
They arise and then pass away.[16]

There are generally two approaches to understanding the relationship between the mind and the brain. By mind we mean the subjective side of things, the full range of lived experience, both conscious and unconscious, including the experience of thought, cognition, memory, desire, emotional states, and even perhaps the sense of transcendence. By brain we refer to the objective side, the physical stuff between our ears and throughout our bodies, with its complex architecture of inter-related neurons and the electro-chemical processes activating, inhibiting, and connecting them.

One approach regards the two as basically identical. In this view all subjective experience not only depends upon but also *consists of* brain activity, and when we have fully mapped out the functions of the brain we will have explained the mind. The other approach considers the mind to be much more than the brain, extending far beyond the merely physical in both scope and capability in ways that the current scientific models either have not yet conceived or are just beginning to glimpse. In this view there are of course parallels between brain activity and subjective states, but the one does not entirely explain the other. Traditionally (both east and west) this non-physical perspective on consciousness involved notions of immaterial soul or higher modes of consciousness that are outside the matrix of physical cause and effect. This view has been steadily retreating before the advances of neuroscience, but recent iterations of it are looking to the new physics for ways of articulating a deeper and more fundamental relationship between mind and matter than formerly imagined.

In Buddhist terms the question comes down to whether all consciousness is conditioned, as the consciousness of the grasping aggregates surely is, or whether consciousness might also be conceived in larger, even unconditioned, terms. Such is the case in some of the later forms of Buddhism, like the Mahayana and Vajrayana, but there are many in the Theravada who see it this way as well. The issue turns on how we construe the word "unconditioned" (asankhata), which is regularly employed as a synonym for nibbana. If everything is conditioned and nibbana is the one state that is unconditioned, then surely awakening consists of at least glimpsing if not deeply experiencing a form of consciousness well beyond conditioned phenomena and thus beyond the mere brain. On the other hand, the term "unconditioned" is most plainly defined only as the absence of greed, hatred, and delusion (as in the Asankhata Samyutta[17]), consciousness is specifically declared to be conditioned,[18] and nowhere, at least in the Pali texts, do we find the (oxymoronic) phrase "unconditioned consciousness."

Either some are making too much of consciousness, or others are making too little of it. As I understand the early teachings, the Buddha was trying to steer us to a middle way of approaching this issue, a way between what he called eternalism and annihilationism.

It is tempting, both in ancient and contemporary tradition, to essentialize consciousness or ascribe to it a status well beyond "that which appears" in experience when a sense object or a mental object is cognized by means of its corresponding organ. The classic expression of this in the literature is the case of a lamp and its light: "Would anyone be speaking rightly who spoke thus: 'While this oil-lamp is burning, its oil, wick, and flame are impermanent and subject to change, but its radiance is permanent, everlasting, eternal, not subject to change?'" "No, venerable sir. Why is that? Because while that oil-lamp is burning, its oil, wick, and flame are impermanent and subject to change, so its radiance must be impermanent and subject to change."[19] If mind is considered to be much more than brain, then we are invoking an ontological category beyond our present capability to express, since all our science is a science of conditioned events. Yes, there is a brave new physics coming into view, but I worry about the tendency to explain what we don't understand in terms of something else we don't understand.

It is equally tempting to want to reduce something we don't understand very well yet (consciousness) to something we do understand (matter). But the inadequacy of our conceptual tools does not necessarily constrain the phenomenon itself. The example that comes to mind from the texts is of the man who inquires about a fire that has just been extinguished "To which direction has the fire gone, the north, south, east, or west?"[20] The problem with simply reducing mind to brain is not only that the teachings about rebirth are challenged, but the scope and promise of awakening seems somehow reduced to accepting one's death rather than transcending it in a remarkable way. Did the Buddha merely die happily, or did he in some important sense pass over life and death and attain the Deathless?

I suspect our challenge lies not in choosing one horn of this dilemma over another, but in learning how to understand consciousness in a new, middle, way. One step toward the center might be to remove the words "merely" from a physical description of brain activity, such that a material explanation might not bring with it a sense that mind is "reduced" to something of lesser value. Another step in from the other side might involve the recognition that mind, if it be conceived as an emergent property arising from the neuronal activity of the brain, nevertheless *virtually* creates a higher order of meaning than anything else in our natural world. Even if consciousness is conditioned, it may still be something very special.

In the early texts the Buddha seems to regard the mind and the brain as fundamentally interdependent, each conditioned equally by the other in experience. He describes it in objective terms, as consisting of impersonal, interdependently arising bases, aggregates, and elements, none of which, because of impermanence, themselves survive from one day to the next, let alone from one life to another. Yet he also describes the incomparable value of engaging, investigating, and understanding the living experience of moment-to-moment consciousness, from the inside, and guides all of us in that enterprise toward an experience of inexpressible transcendent meaningfulness. These two views may not be antithetical.

THIS FATHOM-LONG
CARCASS

The end of the world can never be reached by walking. However, without hav-
ing reached the world's end there is no release from suffering. I declare that it is
in this fathom-long carcass, with its perceptions and thoughts, that there is the
world, the origin of the world, the cessation of the world, and the path leading
to the cessation of the world.[21]

This radical statement attributed to the Buddha constitutes no less than a
Copernican revolution in thought, with far-reaching consequences for our
understanding of the human condition. It redefines "the world" in a way that
flies in the face of both the scientific and the religious traditions of the
West, but which is remarkably well suited to the postmodern views emerging along the cutting edges of the new cognitive and neurological sciences.

We are used to hearing from scientists that "the world" is made of material substances that have coalesced into clumps following their creation and
dispersal by the big bang. These have gradually become more heavy and
diverse and, upon this planet at least, have evolved into living organisms of
increasing complexity. Neural systems then develop among some of these
organisms, generating patterns of electrical and chemical activity that manifest in the phenomenon we call consciousness. This unique physical
process generates a node of subjective experience, allowing each conscious
creature to be "aware" of the material environment it inhabits.

The religious view, shared by most of the Western traditions, comes at
the matter from the other direction. Consciousness is an essential attribute
of spirit or soul, the immaculate creation of an omnipotent maker, and is
given to each individual as a precious gift. The material world, of lesser

ontological importance, is provided as an environment for the soul to inhabit and within which to be tested.

The Buddha of the early Pali texts found difficulties in each of these positions. His critique was that both constitute edifices of conceptual construction, neither of which is verifiable in immediate experience. The scientific model posits a multidimensional world extended in time and space, and looks at most issues from this "objective" perspective. The spiritual view takes for granted the soul as an essential entity, outside the matrix of cause and effect, and the sole authority for this tends to be ancient traditions whose authors are unknown. In each case, says the Buddha, one builds up a "view" of the world based on assumptions, beliefs, or speculations that exceeds anyone's direct personal experience.

The perspective articulated by the Buddha was something very different from either materialism or spiritualism, and might be called an early form of *phenomenology*. What we take to be "the world" is a virtual construction of the human mind and body, woven together of moments of consciousness arising and falling away in an ongoing stream. It is a world of appearances, of phenomena, constructed and imbued with meaning locally by each individual according to patterns learned from, and passed on to, others.

The Buddha seems to accept both the material and the spiritual elements of the other positions, but refuses to put either in a place of primacy. Matter is a condition for the manifestation of consciousness, and consciousness is a condition for any experience of matter. Posing the issue as a choice between whether the world "really exists" out there or is "merely created by the mind" is just too clumsy. It is the interaction of the two that yields the world as we know it, a world consisting of moments of knowing.

From this perspective, the senses of our bodies depend upon material phenomena for their form and for their sustenance, as do the objects that impinge on these senses. But a moment of experience of these objects by means of the senses can only occur when consciousness enters the relationship. Consciousness manifests as the *knowing* of an object by a sense, a process we refer to as *seeing, hearing, smelling, tasting,* or *touching*. It can also generate mental objects from its own memories, perceptions, and symbol-creation capabilities, in which case we say we are *thinking* (in the broadest sense of the term). What is unique about the Buddha's model is that consciousness is not something apart from or independent of a specific moment of knowing—it is conditioned like everything else.

At the level of direct experience manifesting in the immediate moment, the mind and body work together to construct what I have been calling a virtual world. Much of the project of Buddhism has to do with understanding the dynamics and the qualities of this constructed world. It turns out that the enterprise can unfold in skillful or unskillful ways, yielding a world beset by suffering or free from suffering. Stories about the properties of material phenomena, or about the history and purpose of consciousness, are largely irrelevant to the task of understanding the nature of the world—as it appears—and of using that knowledge to skillfully transform our experience.

Returning to the passage with which this chapter began, by saying the end of the world cannot be reached by walking, the Buddha is referring to the concept of the material world extended in space. (This sentiment is amplified in the text on a more mythic scale by the deva Rohitassa, to whom the Buddha is speaking, who says he spent his entire last lifetime running day and night, in strides each as wide as the earth, to reach the end of the world—unsuccessfully.) But one can never understand the nature of suffering, its arising and ceasing, without fully exploring and "reaching the end" of the virtual world constructed by consciousness and the senses, by perceptions and feeling.

This is an enterprise only accomplished by meditation, by the thorough investigation of phenomena, and by treading the Buddhist path—the inner, virtual path—to awakening.

MAKING
THE BEST OF IT

ENSORY INFORMATION hurtles in at our eyeballs at the speed of light, crashes into our eardrums at the speed of sound, and courses through our body and mind as fast as an electrochemical signal can flash from one neuron to the next. And how do we deal with all this data without getting overwhelmed? By blocking out most of it, and stepping down the voltage on what little is left.

The brain freezes the world into discrete mind moments, each capturing a barely adequate morsel of information, then processes these one by one in a rapid linear sequence. The result is a compiled virtual world of experience, more or less patterned on what's "out there," but mostly organized around the needs and limitations of the apparatus constructing it. It is like the brain and its senses are hastily taking a series of snapshots, then stringing them together into a movie we call "the stream of consciousness."

The Buddhists have a pretty good word to describe this system: *delusion*. It doesn't mean we are stupid, only that the mind and body are designed (so to speak) to distort reality in some very fundamental ways. For starters, each moment of consciousness creates an artificial node of stability out of a background that is thoroughly in flux. As the flip-chart of mind moments rapidly unfolds, we weave all sorts of narratives about the way things are, filling in the blanks with various assumptions, projections, and aspirations. Taking these as real, we go on to seek gratification and security to a degree the constructed system cannot support. The ensuing dissatisfaction is organized around the notion of "myself," who is both the one who wishes things were different than they are and the one who suffers when they are not. We are hard-wired, in other words, to misconstrue the nature of reality by obscuring the impermanence, unsatisfactoriness, and selflessness at the heart of it all.

There is another way the amount of data we need to process at any given moment is even further reduced. Most of what comes into the system does not even reach the threshold of consciousness but is relegated below conscious awareness. The precious resource of conscious awareness is generally apportioned only on a "need to know" basis. When first learning a task, such as playing the piano, we have to "think about it" and "try" consciously to make our fingers go where they are supposed to go. But as the right connections are made in the brain and among the muscles of the fingers and hand, the patterns subside into lower levels of consciousness and after a while it feels as if we are playing "automatically."

Because this process works so efficiently, it is not long before most of what we do in our lives can be accomplished without having to be very conscious of it. You would think this frees up our mental energy for some really creative things, but alas this is too seldom the case. More often than not consciousness is used merely to seek out the things that please us and strategize about how to get more of them, or it is used to disparage the things that displease us and to conspire to avoid, ignore, or destroy them. We wind up using our conscious mind to pursue new ways of desiring things to be different than they are, while the unconscious mind is relegated the task of maintaining whatever habits we happened to have stumbled into in previous endeavors to change what was happening. The Buddhists have a good word for this too: *suffering*.

Much of meditation has to do with learning to use consciousness as a tool for transforming our unconscious, where all the underlying dispositions abide. Paradoxically, we can only change what we are not aware of by becoming more aware of something else. That is to say, our unconscious has been conditioned by all sorts of unwholesome patterns of response, and these are used to guide conscious behavior. By definition we are not aware of most of these, but become aware of the suffering they cause in the course of lived experience. By training conscious awareness on an innocuous object such as the breath, we strengthen its ability to open to more and more of the information available to the senses in present time.

As the mind fills with direct sensory experience, which it does when practicing mindfulness of the body, for example, it empties of desire for things to be otherwise than they are. Mindfulness means being present to whatever is happening here and now—when mindfulness is strong, there is no room left in the mind for wanting something else. With less liking and disliking of what arises, there is less pushing and pulling on the world, less defining of the threshold between self and other, resulting in a reduced construction of self. As the influence of self diminishes, suffering diminishes in proportion.

It is natural and inevitable that we are always working with an imperfect model of reality. It makes a difference, however, to understand the limitations of our constructed system, to see more clearly the consequences of it being both unskillfully and skillfully employed, and to use this knowledge to maximize the well-being available for ourselves and all those around us.

And the Buddhist word for this is *wisdom*.

UNREAL IMAGINATION EXISTS

ONE OF MY FAVORITE EXPRESSIONS from Buddhist literature is the three-word opening line of a late Sanskrit text that nicely captures the subtle, paradoxical view of reality so unique to Buddhist thought. Attributed to Maitreya (a scholar by that name, not the coming Buddha) as the author of a Yogacara text called the *Madhyantavibhaga* the phrase is *abhuta-parikalpo'sti*, and translates something like "unreal imagination exists." Let's explore some of the ideas lying behind this intriguing phrase.

The middle word, *parikalpa*, is the noun, so let's start there. It's rooted in a term ($\sqrt{klrip}$)[22] that most immediately means "capability" or "feasibility"; with the prefix *pari-* added it takes on the sense of something contrived, determined, or invented. Here it refers to the understanding that the mind and body are constructing a world of experience—each moment—out of the raw data of sensory input. Others might see this as the functioning of a conscious spiritual essence, but Buddhists regard every moment of consciousness as a synthetic event that is cobbled together out of presenting conditions, only to pass away as those conditions change to make way for the creation of a new configuration. The name given to this process here is *parikalpa*—a constructed, arranged, worked-out fabrication of some feasible or approximate version of things that we can take as a plausible semblance of reality for the purposes of stumbling from one moment to another. Such is the nature of human experience, all wishful thinking or projected hopes aside. It is an illusion, the outcome of a potent imagination.

The first word of the phrase is an adjective, describing this product of our imagination as unreal, not truly existing, not grounded upon any ontological foundation. The verbal root "√bhu" simply means "to be," so the negative form of that, abhuta, quite strongly says that the object in question does not *really* exist. This is a remarkable insight, one that pulls the ground out from under almost all other forms of human understanding of the ultimate. Existence is one of the three primary definitions of god and soul in Hinduism (sat-cit-ananda: existence-consciousness-bliss), and for the Buddhists to say that such a reassuring reality does not underlie the functioning of the mind and body was as challenging to the Buddha's contemporaries as it is to us today. Yet this is what he saw on the night of his awakening—the world has no abiding essence.

The third word is a verb, another form of "to be" (√as = asti), and simply declares that this imaginative act we call ourselves and our world, which ultimately has no basis, nevertheless "exists." That is to say it appears, it is an event that occurs, it arises again after it passes away, it is present to experience, it serves as an object of awareness. This third act of the play takes us away from the theoretical and into the practical realm of meditation and daily life. *Even though* the mind is synthesizing a virtual world, and *even though* this imaginative connivance is ultimately ungrounded in anything "out there," it *nevertheless* is phenomenologically present. We have the option of paying careful attention to the flow of experience, and thereby of participating intimately in the manifestations of consciousness. When such conscious engagement is tempered with the first two insights, the insubstantiality and imperfection of it all, we gain back at least as much as we have lost. The bird in hand is a rich unfolding of phenomenological texture and nuance; the two in the bush, not worth pursuing, are merely conceptual urges to feel grounded in something transcendent.

It is often taken for granted that all religion points beyond the here and now to something wholly other, and that the value of this is entirely derived from the value of that. I think the Buddha had a very different view (echoes to the contrary in later tradition notwithstanding), and this view is particularly suited to the postmodern world we are beginning to inhabit. The ontological ground has been pulled out from under us by every discovery of the new sciences over the last century, and increasingly isolated islands of religious bedrock are surrounded by shifting sands of pluralism. The conventional wisdom has always been that we would be lost without some kind of transcendent grounding, and that human values, aspirations, and responsibilities would flounder without divine guidance.

The Buddha appears to have seen it the other way around. Clinging to a rock while being battered by waves only causes damage, while letting go and learning to swim freely in the swirling waters can result in a great sense of meaning and well-being. We can accept the fact that our world-building apparatus is imperfect (*parikalpa*), and even that our world and our selves are not ultimately real (*abhuta*), while at the same time learning to pay ever-closer attention to the flow of experience that is presenting itself to awareness (*asti*). We can rely upon the self-organizing principles of nature to build for ourselves a meaningful world, as long as we take care to do so in healthy rather than unhealthy ways. Having seen the empty nature of it all a long time ago, Buddhists went on to organize a way of life around such qualities as kindness, compassion, truthfulness, and understanding—above all, around practices of heightened awareness, because these are the mental states that optimize experience.

I understand that everything I know and do is a product of *imagination*, and I can accept without difficulty that it is ultimately *unreal*, but I'm glad it *exists* and I will engage with that existence with as much conscious awareness as I can possibly muster. This is plenty to work with and inspires me to make the very best of what is present for myself, for those around me, and for the collective whole. The future well-being of us all, said the Buddha a long time ago, lies in the direction of less conceptual attachment to views and more mindful awareness of phenomena.

This simple phrase can serve as a good reminder of that. Unreal imagination exists.

IN THE BLINK
OF AN EYE

HOW FAR AWAY from one another are suffering and the end of suffering? In truth, the distance can be traversed in the blink of an eye.
That is the good news delivered to us by the Buddha in the *Indriyabhavana Sutta*, the very last text of the *Majjhima Nikaya*.[23]

In an exchange with a Brahmin student named Uttara, the teaching
begins with a description of something universal in human experience:

> When a person sees a form with the eye . . . hears a sound with
> the ear . . . smells an odor with the nose . . . tastes a flavor with
> the tongue . . . touches a tangible with the body . . . or cognizes
> a mind-object with the mind, there arises in him what is agree-
> able, there arises what is disagreeable, there arises what is both
> agreeable and disagreeable.

Perhaps you have noticed this. It is entirely natural that all sensory experience is accompanied by a feeling tone of pleasure or pain (or in many
cases a feeling that is neither pleasant nor painful, but viscerally immediate
nonetheless). This is just the way we are hard-wired as sentient beings:
feeling is an intrinsic component of all experience.

However, in response to (and co-arising with) this feeling tone, we also
quite naturally seem to find pleasurable experience agreeable and painful
experience disagreeable. In many cases the same object can be both agreeable in some ways and disagreeable in others. As embodied creatures, we

find ourselves with reflexes to pursue what is pleasant and to avoid what is painful. This is where our troubles begin.

Such primitive programming has no doubt helped us survive long enough to develop the higher brain functions unique to humans, but evidence is mounting—in the shape of a world consumed by the fires of greed, hatred, and delusion—that these same instincts are becoming obsolete and counterproductive to our well-being. One of the great insights of the Buddha is that the very mechanism of desire, by means of which we crave some aspects of experience and reject other aspects, is the fundamental cause of suffering.

This too is just the way it is: suffering occurs. So what tools do we have at our disposal to cope with the situation? As mammals we are also endowed with innate impulses toward generosity, kindness, compassion, and cooperation that help counteract and at times override the more primal, selfish instincts. More significantly, we also have a protruding prefrontal cortex enabling introspection, self-reflection, and mindfulness. Encouraging us to put this organ to work, the Buddha goes on to say:

> One is aware of this: "There has arisen in me what is agreeable, there has arisen what is disagreeable, there has arisen what is both agreeable and disagreeable."

This observation might not sound like much, but it is a huge step. Bringing awareness to the inner life, to the phenomenological texture of experience, allows light to shine in the darkness. Seeing what arises and passes away in the mind and body each moment allows what we experience to become something known and understood, rather than something shaped entirely by invisible unconscious conditioning. Such mindfulness provides the necessary prerequisite for the next transformative step pointed to by the Buddha: insight into the nature of phenomena.

> "But that is conditioned, gross, dependently arisen; while this is peaceful, this is sublime, namely, equanimity." The agreeable that arose, the disagreeable that arose, and the both agreeable and disagreeable that arose cease in him and equanimity is established.

One can discern, with the faculty Buddhists call *wisdom*, that all experience is shaped within a milieu of cause and effect. The "disagreeableness" that has arisen is merely a mental attitude of aversion, coagulating around a particular feeling of displeasure, which co-arises with the cognizing of a particular sensory object. The attitude is a product of one's dispositions, which are themselves nothing more than patterns of learned responses that have built up during a lifetime (or more) of acting and reacting in the world.

Such a breakthrough in understanding allows for a dramatic and immediate liberation of the mind from the coercion of desire—both the desire to hold on to what is deemed agreeable and the desire to push away what is disagreeable. For at least one moment, the moment of insight, desire is replaced by equanimity. Equanimity here does not mean disconnection or neutral feeling, but a much more profound state that allows one to remain imperturbable in the face of even the strongest feelings. When one realizes that the arising feeling is one thing, while the attitude generated in response to it is something else entirely, the chain of compulsive causation is broken and a moment of freedom is born.

One can now choose to respond differently, and the agreeable/disagreeable attitude that forms the warp and woof of our suffering can be replaced by something capable of embracing both pleasure and pain without reaction. Whatever arises is okay. There is no need to hold on to some things while pushing others away. Serene, yet radically intimate with experience, we can, like the Buddha, abide in any moment with the hint of a smile on our lips.

This might sound like a distant ideal, but the Buddha suggests it is accessible here and now:

> Just as a man with good sight, having opened his eyes might shut them or having shut his eyes might open them, so too, concerning anything at all, the agreeable that arose, the disagreeable that arose, and the both agreeable and disagreeable that arose cease just as quickly, just as rapidly, just as easily, and equanimity is established.

He makes it sound so easy. All it takes is a gentle shift in attitude, a simple letting go of liking and not liking, an opening to the moment as it is rather than as we wish it would be.

With sufficient understanding, the journey from suffering to freedom can be made in the blink of an eye.

SECTION 4
THE PRACTICE

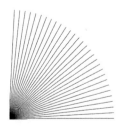

ONE THING
AT A TIME

Don't go back over what has past,
Nor yearn for what is yet to be.
What has past has been abandoned,
And the future is not yet here.
The state arising here and now—
see it with insight as it is! [24]

When the Buddha says, "I know of no single thing more conducive to great harm than an unrestrained mind," [25] I think he is referring to the current penchant for multitasking. When the mind tries to do several things at once, it does not do any of them very well. This is an empirical fact attested by numerous experiments, and is easily demonstrated for oneself: try simultaneously texting a message while driving, guided by your GPS through an unfamiliar neighborhood, while catching the latest sports scores on the radio and discussing some recent relationship difficulty with your partner.

It is not that the mind is incapable of such feats of parallel processing, it's just not a very healthy thing to do. One image in the Pali texts [26] compares the flow of consciousness to a mountain stream flowing swiftly downhill. If there are several outlets through which the water is dispersed, then when it reaches the plain it will be little more than a trickle. Mental energy is finite, and our mind is diminished in direct proportion to how much its attention is fractured. The problem is not so much attention deficit as it is attention *dispersion*, when the available attention is spread thin. Just like water spreading out to cover a surface, the wider the expanse the shallower the depth. By trying to do many things at once we are training the mind to process information in ways that may well be effective and even become habitual, but the price to be paid for this is no longer being deeply aware of what we are doing.

Of course being deeply aware of what we are doing is the very crux of the Buddhist teaching, which is why the practice of meditation is so important for unifying and consolidating the mind. The Buddha also said, "I know of no single thing more conducive to great welfare than a developed mind."[27] Concentration practice, known as *samadhi*, consists of gathering together (the prefix *sam-*) and placing (the root √*dha*) the mind upon (the middle *a*) an object of the senses or upon a mental object. We do this all the time reflexively, but in Buddhist practice we are invited to do so with deliberate intention, with sustaining energy, and with consistency over multiple mind moments.

It is natural for the mind to resist such discipline, and to wander off to any aspect of experience that is new, unusual, or apparently more interesting. We did not survive in nature by ignoring incoming stimuli, and like birds or chipmunks are more accustomed to glancing around constantly, attentive to both threat and opportunity. But we are no longer crouching in a hostile natural environment, and the states to which our mind restlessly turns in the meditation hall are generally internally constructed threats and imaginary opportunities. The cultivation of mental focus, the consistent return to a primary object, and the settling into ever deeper states of tranquility has the effect of gradually reigning in the mind's random wandering and settles it down in a way that gathers and consolidates the power of awareness.

Each moment of consciousness is a precious gift. Awareness itself is the primary currency of the human condition, and as such it is inherently of immense value and deserves to be spent carefully. Merely sitting quietly in a serene environment, letting go of the various petty disturbances that roil and diminish consciousness, and experiencing as fully as possible the poignancy of this fleeting moment—this is an enterprise of deep intrinsic value, an aesthetic experience beyond words. The more unified, stable, luminous, and attentive the mind is at this moment, the more profound the experience.

Our contemporary view of consciousness is so different from this, so much less. It is as if the accomplishment of mere tasks is of primary value, while the quality of awareness with which these tasks are undertaken is irrelevant. One can hurtle through the day doing this, that, and the other thing, often simultaneously, with great busyness and pressure, only to relax in the evening by trying to keep up with images that flash across the screen multiple times per second. For many of us, the deep states of tranquil alertness of which the mind is capable are entirely unknown.

Yes, the chattering, cavorting, cacophonous monkey mind is capable of clever deeds and great mischief, and these things are not entirely without value. But the mind is also capable of settling down, gathering its power, and turning its gaze upon itself, and in such instances it can come to know itself deeply. Buddhists call this gaining wisdom, and this too is a valuable thing to do.

More importantly, perhaps, it is a healthy thing to do. It is now well known that a restful body is healthier than a body in constant states of stress. It is becoming better known that a restful mind is more healthy than a mind beset with anxiety, compulsion, addiction, and other agitating states. It may even turn out to be the case that a restful society is healthier than one beset with tension, prejudice, exploitation, and war. I hope we have a chance to find out some day.

Meanwhile, peace is accessible. This too is an empirically demonstrable fact: try turning off the radio, the phone, the computer, and the TV; sit comfortably in a quiet place, relaxing the body and mind; mindfully breathing in, mindfully breathing out, and abandon—just for now—any thought or response that tends to disburse and divide your awareness. Let go, for the moment, the impulse for sensory gratification, hold off annoyance toward what you don't like, settle down any restlessness in mind and body, stir up energy when you feel sluggish, and postpone thinking over any doubts you may have. As you do this successfully for several moments in a row, you will find the mind gradually becoming more tranquil, more focused, more clear, and more powerful. The Buddha might have said, "I know of no single thing more healthy than doing one thing at a time."

HERE AND NOW

Y OU DON'T HAVE TO have read a lot of Buddhist texts to know that consciousness comes streaming through six doors, each one framed by one of six cognizing organs (the five senses and the mind) and opening onto one of six cognized objects. Just take a moment to explore the field of experience, and you will see that you know things in six different ways. One sphere of knowing is visual, another is auditory. Seeing and hearing are two different activities, each using separate parts of the body and distinct processing centers in the brain. If you cycle between one and the other, you will know quite directly what is happening right now in the environment around you. Moment after moment you will see and then hear, hear and then see, some specific input of data flowing through these two sense doors.

The same is happening with the knowing of smells, tastes, and tactile sensations. Each involves a different mode of consciousness, and each translates some aspect of the environment into a different experiential language. Consciousness is singular in the sense that it is all just knowing, but this knowing manifests variously as particular organs respond to particular objects. In classical Buddhist thought these variations are called the five strands of sense experience (*kama-guna*), and they appear to the mindful meditator as a stream of changing experience.

Here is the thing: these five sense inputs can only access information that is happening in the present moment. They are each connected to specialized receptors at the end of nerve bundles, which are responding to real-time stimuli with present moment representation. You cannot directly experience a touch that took place years ago, nor hear a bell that has not yet rung. When we appear to do this, by remembering past experience or by imagining future experience, we are using the sixth mode of consciousness, the mind door. When a mental object (which covers a wide territory of memories, thoughts, plans, computations, and so much more) is known by the mind, a moment of mental consciousness occurs. This is "thinking" in the broadest sense of the word.

Mental experience is similar to sense experience insofar as it, too, is happening in the present moment. But an important difference is that the *content* of a mental experience may go well beyond the present moment to represent something far into the past or future. The thought you are having right now may be of something you did yesterday or anticipate doing tomorrow. It does not work the same way for the other senses. You can form a mental image of something that happened in the past, and that mental image might even draw upon some of the brain's visual apparatus as you appear to "see" it in your "mind's eye," but you do not see it in the same way you see an object before you in the present moment.

This ability to think about the past and the future yields tremendous learning, planning, and problem-solving skills, but it also comes with at least one major drawback. It is possible for people to dwell almost exclusively in the mental mode and have very little direct contact with the senses. Yes, one might check in with the other senses enough to navigate the physical world, but often as little as necessary to keep one's bearings and provide basic input for the mind's proliferations. As the human animal lives less in a rapidly changing natural environment filled with sensual nuance and permeated with danger, and more in a synthetic world with all its parameters defined, it becomes more adaptive to rely heavily on the mental realm at the expense of the senses.

But for many people this becomes a trap. What happens when you can't stop spinning out threatening alternative futures, or you cannot help reliving past traumas? What happens when the pendulum swinging from past to future becomes a fiendish carnival ride you can neither slow down nor escape? At a certain point one can feel driven by the mind's habit of churning over various scenarios, and this often results in a great deal of suffering.

The solution offered by the Buddhist tradition is systematic training in attending to the senses. The first foundation of mindfulness, for example, guides the meditator exclusively to the body door. Become aware of physical sensations—whether those associated with breathing, walking, or almost any other activity—and when the mind averts toward thinking, as it will surely do often, simply redirect awareness back to bodily sensations. It sounds simple enough, yet it has a huge impact.

The reason this is effective is that the mind can be aware of only one thing at a time. If it is a thought, then there is no sense cognition; but in a moment of sense cognition, there are no thoughts. At first, there may be far more mind-moments of mental cognition than of sense cognition in the stream of consciousness; but over time, as the practice of mindfulness of the body develops, one can actually have multiple consecutive moments of sense awareness uninterrupted by "thinking about" what one is sensing. To those who habitually think too much, this is experienced as blissful relief. And it is an essential starting point for growth in understanding.

The Buddha offers an image of the mind like a water jug. If it is half-full of water, Mara—the personification of delusion in Buddhist mythic imagery—can gain access and cause all sorts of mischief. This happens when one senses the world with half of one's available awareness, and thinks about it with the other half. Mara, a trickster figure, represents the unseen (i.e., unconscious) neurotic habitual tendencies that usually direct mental chatter. But if the water jug is full to the brim, Mara can gain no access. Conscious awareness is fully engaged, but with direct sense experience rather than with mental narrative.

By filling up the senses, one empties out the mind. With the peace that ensues from quieting the mind in this way, Dharma investigation can begin.

TUG OF WAR

IMAGINE WHAT WOULD HAPPEN if you took six lengths of rope and tied each to one of six creatures: a snake, a crocodile, a bird, a dog, a jackal, and a monkey. Then tie the loose ends of all these ropes together into a big knot—and let the knot go. What do you think would happen? Each of these animals would pull in a different direction, trying to return to its favorite haunts. The snake would slither toward its nest in the anthill, the crocodile would pull for the river, the bird would fly up into the air, the dog would head to the village, the jackal to the charnel ground, and the monkey would scamper for the trees. Can you picture such a scene?

The Buddha tells this story[28] to illustrate the state of the undisciplined mind, wherein each of the six senses (eye, ear, nose, tongue, body, and mind) is drawn to its own domain and to its customary feeding grounds in pursuit of pleasure. He describes this situation as dwelling with a limited mind, wherein a person has no freedom whatsoever. The solution he offers is to drive a stake through the central knot into the ground, thus binding all six animals to the spot. The stake is a designation for mindfulness of the body, and it is said to be the means of attaining freedom.

How can this be? Surely this is turning on its head our ordinary notion of freedom and offering something thoroughly counterintuitive, if not downright paradoxical. Usually we consider ourselves free only when we can do what we want, and would consider being tethered to a post to be the worst kind of bondage. But let's look at the image a bit closer to try and figure out what the Buddha has in mind here.

Each of these six creatures feels itself to be free if it can go where it wants, but in fact each is bound in several ways. First, it is compelled by instinct to pursue pleasure and avoid pain; next, it generally only knows to seek its gratification in accustomed places; and finally it can only make headway toward its desired object if it gains a temporary advantage in the tug-of-war with the others. Before long each animal will expend its energy in the struggle, and will eventually be dragged around by whichever is the strongest (my money, by the way, is on the crocodile).

The six senses of the human mind and body are bound by an internal constraint more compelling than any rope or stake, insofar as they will always pull in the direction of agreeable objects and regard disagreeable objects as repulsive. From the Buddha's perspective the freedom to pursue this compulsion is an illusory sense of freedom concocted by a constricted and profoundly deluded mind. It's a bit like telling an addict he is free to stop using drugs if he wants, or suggesting to an inmate he is free to go wherever he wishes in his cell.

Mindfulness practice offers the restraint necessary to overcome the tug of desire upon the senses. As we notice the mind wandering off to explore a gratifying train of thought, or as we notice the body's urging to nudge ourselves into a more comfortable position, we gently abandon the impulse and return attention to the primary object of awareness. We do this again and again, until the mind becomes content being fully present with what is manifesting here and now in the field of experience, rather than rushing off for some other form of stimulation. As the mind settles down it becomes considerably more powerful, and thus more empowered.

The story told by the Buddha ends in a lovely picture of all six animals lying down contentedly in one another's company, no longer exerting themselves, no longer yearning for something else. Similarly, when the tugging of sense desire and aversion has been quieted, when restlessness and sluggishness have been balanced out, and when doubts are put aside for a time, the mind is able to attend to experience more openly and with much greater freedom. With the senses no longer struggling to reach pleasing forms and no longer regarding unpleasing forms as repulsive, the mind is able to see more clearly what is actually arising and falling away.

In this mode the mind is said to be *unlimited*, and is capable of experiencing a greater freedom through wisdom. Its freedom comes not from the license to broadly explore a shallow terrain, defined by its likes and dislikes, but rather from the ability to shake off the constraints of desire altogether and plunge deeply into investigating the field of experience as it is. It turns out that *what* one sees, hears, smells, tastes, touches, or thinks is not as important as *how* one does so.

We are used to thinking of freedom as being free to do what we want, but the Buddha sees real freedom as being free from wanting. We tend to think of the post as the fetter, and freedom as being able to obtain agreeable objects of sense—whereas the Buddha considers the *pursuit of pleasure* to be the fetter, and mindfulness offers us a chance to break free of its bonds.

Perhaps internal freedom is ultimately more valuable than external freedom.

CHANGING
YOUR MIND

THE BUDDHA MADE a big deal of the distinction between wholesome
and unwholesome states of mind. Most religious and philosophical traditions probably share this point of view to some extent. But the
Buddha was unique in offering a detailed way of understanding how and
why the mind manifests as it does in any given moment. There are patterns
of cause and effect that can be seen in experience and traced over time to
explain the dynamics at work shaping each moment of consciousness. The
word for this is *karma*, and it does *not* mean fate.

Moreover, the Buddha offered a simple and universal method for transforming mind states from unwholesome to wholesome. This is important
because, as the very first verse of the *Dhammapada* says, we become what we
think. Every thought, emotion, intention, attitude, or aspiration is shaping
how ensuing experience will unfold. This means that every single moment
of consciousness is a moment of practice, whether we like it or not. We are
practicing to become ourselves. The important question is really just how
much we want to participate in the process.

As I understand his teachings, the Buddha was expounding what we
might call a post-Copernican revolution. The world really does revolve
around us, insofar as our mind is the instrument for the local construction
of meaning. Left unattended, the mind will tend to organize around greed,
hatred, and delusion, and will create unwholesome states that "obstruct wisdom and lead away from awakening."[29] The solution to the problem, at
least according to the earliest strata of Buddhist tradition, is to learn the

healthy skill of transforming such mind states. A simple method of doing so is laid out in the *Anumana Sutta*[30] of the *Majjhima Nikaya*.

STEP ONE. *Notice: "A person [with unwholesome qualities] is displeasing and disagreeable to me."* This is a generic way of stating it. The text actually offers a long list of specific qualities, such as anger, hate, contempt, deceit, and arrogance, within the square brackets. I'm sure we can all come up with our own unique list of unwholesome qualities we find displeasing in others. Notice that the emphasis here is not upon the other person ("They have such unwholesome qualities!"), but upon one's own response in the moment ("I am experiencing displeasure in the face of this behavior").

STEP TWO. *Infer: "If I were to have unwholesome qualities, I would be displeasing and disagreeable to others."* This is the pivotal moment of the process, for it turns attention toward oneself rather than placing it upon the other. It is almost automatic in our culture to impugn others for their behavior, and this would normally result in blaming or trying to rectify the other: "If only they would not be like that, I'd be okay." Here it is rather "If only *I* would not be like that, *they* would be okay." The subtlety of the Buddha's insight here is not only that transforming one's own inner states is the most direct path to happiness, but also, because of the laws of karmic interdependence, such a change will have the additional effect of transforming others.

STEP THREE. *A person who knows this should arouse his mind thus: "I shall not have unwholesome qualities."* This step involves undertaking the resolve to change the qualities of one's own mind. What a radical idea in an era that so often takes it for granted that the world should be modified to meet our desires long before we should change ourselves. Opening to things just as they are is a more popular aspect of Buddhist practice than the subsequent step of understanding the nature of what is arising and letting go of it if it is unwholesome. Yet this is precisely where right view, right intention, right mindfulness, and right effort converge in treading the Buddha's path to awakening.

STEP FOUR. *A person should review himself thus: "Do I have unwholesome qualities?"* Mindfulness meditation provides access to the landscape of inner experience. Like fondling the beads on a necklace slowly slipping through the fingers, one learns to savor each moment of consciousness and look closely at its texture and nuance. As insight grows and wisdom deepens, the sense of what is wholesome and unwholesome emerges gradually and intuitively. It is not a discursive or judgmental process, but it does require rigorous honesty.

STEP FIVE. *When he reviews himself, if he knows: "I have unwholesome qualities," then he should make an effort to abandon those unwholesome states.* It is inevitable that one will discern unwholesome qualities of mind when one looks openly on what is actually occurring in experience. As many people remark, meditation can be a most humbling experience. But there is never any blame for simply noticing what is there. When something unwholesome is seen in oneself, the determination to change it will arise in proportion to one's understanding. How one goes about changing it, however, is a matter of great importance. Accepting what is unwholesome out of attachment, or acting it out in an attempt to purge it, will just strengthen that quality of mind. Similarly, trying to overlook or suppress it will simply postpone and fortify the problem. Abandoning involves first seeing it for what it is, then recognizing the conditions that contribute to clinging to it, and finally gently releasing one's hold on the unwholesome quality— one moment at a time.

STEP SIX. *When he reviews himself, if he knows: "I have no unwholesome qualities," then he can abide happy and glad, training day and night in* *wholesome states.* There will also be times when a review of consciousness reveals no unwholesome qualities of mind. This is good. It is entirely appropriate in such cases to experience happiness and gladness.

The discourse ends with an image suggesting a process of mental purification: "Just as when a woman—or a man—who is youthful and fond of ornaments, on viewing the image of her own face in a clear bright mirror or in a basin of clear water, sees a smudge or a blemish on it, she makes an effort to remove it; but if she sees no smudge or blemish on it, she becomes glad." I suspect both our personal lives and our collective world would be far better off if we cared for our inner states as fastidiously as we do the outer appearance.

CALM IN THE FACE
OF ANGER

IN THE SAKKA CHAPTER of the *Samyutta Nikaya*,[31] the Buddha teaches, as he often did, by means of a parable; this is one that remains as relevant today as it was in ancient India. The story addresses the issue of what a strong person is to do if insulted, attacked, or otherwise provoked by someone weaker. It could, however, just as easily pertain to how a mighty nation might respond to the provocations of a smaller nation or the threats of a criminal.

The Buddha tells of a great battle set in mythological times between the gods and the demons. In the end, the demons were defeated and their leader, Vepacitti, was bound by his four limbs and neck and brought before Sakka, lord of the gods. There, we are told, Vepacitti "abused and reviled [Sakka] with rude, harsh words." (The commentary elaborates upon these insults, and this makes for some very entertaining reading.) Yet Sakka remained calm, regarding his prisoner with mindful compassion. Sakka's charioteer Matali was puzzled by this response, and a poetic debate ensued. Let's listen in:

> *Matali:* Could it be you're afraid, Sakka,
> Or weak that you forebear like this,
> Though hearing such insulting words
> From the mouth of Vepacitti?

Sakka: I am neither afraid nor weak,
Yet I forebear Vepacitti.
How is it one who knows, like me,
Would get provoked by such a fool?

Matali: More angry will a fool become
If no one puts a stop to him.
So let the wise restrain the fool
By the use of a mighty stick.

Sakka: This is the only thing, I deem,
That will put a stop to the fool:
Knowing well the other's anger,
One is mindful and remains calm.

Matali: This very forbearance of yours,
Sakka, I see as a mistake.
For when a fool reckons like this,
"From fear of me he does forebear,"
The dolt will come on stronger still—
Like a bull the more that one flees.

Sakka: Let him think whatever he wants:
"From fear of me he does forebear."
Among ideals and highest goods
None better than patience is found . . .

At issue in this discussion are two opposing models of human nature, as well as two correspondingly different strategies for responding to attack. Matali's approach relies upon the exercise of power to restrain and punish. To act otherwise can only be an indication of fear or weakness. If an adversary senses a hint of either, the argument goes, it will only make him bolder and more aggressive.

Sakka takes a broader view, one grounded in wisdom, patience, and calm.

In his first verse he points out that his forbearance is an expression of his understanding. Knowing how the causes of anger and hatred are rooted in toxic underlying dispositions, and knowing the unwholesome effects these have on mental states when unleashed, he is able to see clearly both the sources of Vepacitti's anger and the harm that comes with venting it. Would one who understands these things allow oneself to be diminished by being pulled off-center and goaded into a comparable expression of anger?

Freedom means being able to choose how we respond to things. When wisdom is not well developed, it can be easily circumvented by the provocations of others. In such cases we might as well be animals or robots. If there is no space between an insulting stimulus and its immediate conditioned response—anger—then we are in fact under the control of others. Mindfulness opens up such a space, and when wisdom is there to fill it one is capable of responding with forbearance. It's not that anger is repressed; anger never arises in the first place.

In his second verse, Sakka makes the further point that absorbing someone's anger without pushing back on it will eventually exhaust the anger. We all know from personal experience how the fire of anger can be fueled as it is hurled back and forth between people, growing in intensity and in its potential for doing harm. This will happen when there is a strong attachment to the sense of self, when there is someone who is insulted and feels wounded, or someone who launches his or her own attack in response. Once again, Sakka points out the importance of "knowing" the anger of the other rather than discounting or ignoring it. But this knowing needs to be *mindful* and *calm* if it is to siphon off and dissipate the anger. If there is no one to accept the anger that is offered, as in the person who truly shares the non-self insights of the Buddha, it will find no place to land and will gain no footing.

The final verse has Sakka reiterating the importance of *patience*, and the value of adhering to what one knows to be beneficial. According to Buddhist teaching, each of us constructs a virtual world of local phenomenal experience, moment to moment, as the mind and the body process sense data. The quality of intention manifesting in this field of experience is a matter of great importance, for it shapes who we are and who we become. From this perspective the views and opinions of Vepacitti are of no consequence to Sakka, whose well-being—that is, his higher good—is better served by maintaining the wholesome influence of patience during all the moments Vepacitti might be hurling abuse at him.

Such inspiring behavior is also rooted in compassion. As the final verses of this exchange attest, calm in the face of anger is motivated as much by concern for the other person as for oneself. Since anger is harmful, helping others let go of their anger by not responding in kind contributes to their healing. What would it take for us, individually or collectively, to exemplify the wisdom of forbearance?

It is indeed a fault for one
Who returns anger for anger;
Not giving anger for anger,
One wins a double victory.
He behaves for the good of both:
Himself and the other person.
Knowing well the other's anger,
He is mindful and remains calm.
In this way he is healing both:
Himself and the other person.
The people who think "He's a fool,"
Just don't understand the Dharma.[32]

SECTION 5
UNDERSTANDING
THE TEACHINGS

INTERCONNECTED . . .
OR NOT?

W HEN I LOOK UP the word "connected" in my dictionary, I find synonyms such as "bound," "fastened," and "attached." Last I heard, these were not considered a good thing in Buddhism. So why do we hear so much about "interconnectedness" these days? Was the Buddha really teaching us that all things are interconnected?

The explanation usually given is that this is what is meant by dependent origination. But is it? As sometimes happens, I think in using this term we are seizing upon a notion from the Western tradition that comes easily to hand, but which misses the nuance of the Buddha's teaching. The traditional term in the exegesis of the commentaries for such an idea—a definition that is close to the truth but is not the truth—is "near enemy." Called "enemy" because it hinders us from properly understanding the concept at hand, a near enemy can be contrasted with a definition that is obviously off the mark, a "far enemy." A near enemy is more insidious, because it seems like a plausible—even desirable—definition, but it nevertheless leads us astray.

My concern about the word "interconnected" is that it rests upon a spatial image suggesting a relationship between two or more things. It tends to be used as an adjective, describing the quality of nouns. Some person, place, or thing is connected or joined to some other person, place, or thing. And when used in its fullest sense, it conjures the image of a great, overarching reality that encompasses and embraces all things. This idea is a cornerstone of Western thought, from the *Logos* of the classical philosopher, to the Great Chain of Being of the Christian theologian, to the Unified Field of the contemporary materialist. On these grounds alone it is worthy of some suspicion as a viable means of conveying uniquely Buddhist ideas.

Buddhist thought is deeply rooted in *process thinking*, wherein the dynamics of the flux are more significant than the temporary structures taking shape and arising within it. From this perspective, *becoming* is too relentlessly changing to ever coalesce into *being*. Dependent origination is more of an adverb, describing how events co-occurring or sequenced in time unfold in relation to one another, than an adjective describing the qualities of a person, place, or thing. Events are shaped by multiple causal factors as they arise in each moment of constructed experience, and the patterns informing this building of the world can be discerned by careful introspection. This is a very different idea than the interconnectedness of all things.

At the cutting edge of human awareness, when the mind is focused skillfully on the birthing of phenomena, there is nothing formed enough to connect with anything. Meditation accesses the flow of experience, upon whose leading edge our world and our self gets formed. The Buddha is inviting us to notice how that process is shaped and influenced by a host of conditions unique to that moment. The language itself (which we'll look at in more detail in the next chapter) is describing a fluid event: "When this occurs, that comes to be; from the arising of this, that also arises. And when this no longer occurs, that comes to an end; from the cessation of this, that also ceases."[33] In the teaching of dependent origination, the Buddha is showing us something very profound about the *process* of becoming.

By contrast, the teaching that "all things are interconnected" is a derivative conceptual construction—lovely, to be sure—but after all, just an idea. I can picture Huineng, the illiterate Sixth Patriarch of Zen, retorting "There are no things, anyway! Let alone any connection between them . . ." I suspect that even the lovely Buddhist simile, Indra's net, would more usefully be translated as Indra's network. The essence of the imagery is the mutual reflection of every jewel in the infinite facets of every other jewel, not in some knotted-together causal scaffolding binding the gems together. Now that we have a wireless network available to us as a paradigm, perhaps its time to retire the fisherman's snare.

I understand the intention behind using the word *interconnected*. If every act tainted by greed or hatred creates and reinforces an illusory sense of self by its "holding on" or "pushing away," and if this falsely constructed self becomes a source of alienation and suffering, then surely the elimination of the "separate self" will result in awakening to a much wider picture of reality. All this is true, but when the little word *separate* is added, it suggests that what one opens to is a *non-separate* self. I think the early Buddha would consider this to be just trading a problem for a much bigger problem.

The quandary of the human condition is not that we are connected to too small an object and need to connect instead to a larger object. Rather it is that the very mechanism of connectivity—attachment—is inherently a cause of suffering. All connections are limiting because by nature, and often unwittingly, they follow the channels of our desires. We want to connect with what is beautiful and gratifying in ourselves, in others, and in the world, but are less enthusiastic about connecting with evil, with cruelty, and with disease. The webs we spin are by and large the projection of our desires into the space we inhabit, and more often than not are meant to snare the objects of our heart's content or protect us from pain.

The Buddha is not telling us to be *dis*connected in the sense of uncaring or selfish—quite the contrary—but he is pointing out something very subtle about human nature. Perhaps what we need is to coin a new word, something like *internonattachedness*. By all means let's share this universe with everyone and everything else inhabiting it, but let's maybe learn to do it in a way that allows things to be more naturally as they are. We'll probably find here a more authentic intimacy.

There is nothing inherently connected about dependently co-arising phenomena. They are merely arising together in experience. The question is how will we hold ourselves in the midst of this process? The more *interconnected* we become, the more bound in the net of conditioned phenomena we may find ourselves. I think the Buddha was pointing a way out of all this, but it is not through getting further connected. It has more to do with getting *less connected*, less entangled, and less attached.

INTERDEPENDENCE

O NE OF THE SIMPLEST yet most profound things attributed to the Buddha in the Pali Canon is the general statement of interdependent origination:

When there is this, there is that,
When there is not this, there is not that.
From the arising of this, that arises.
From the ceasing of this, that ceases.[34]

There are so many ways it can be found meaningful. First and foremost, it expresses the importance of causation for the Buddha, who states very clearly that everything happens in causal, and therefore understandable, patterns. Nothing happens by chance; nothing happens for no reason; and nothing happens simply because a deity wills it. One of the more famous short summaries of the teachings is a verse that brought his two chief disciples to the Dharma: "Whatever things develop from a cause, the Buddha has declared both their cause and their cessation."[35]

Moreover, the general statement of causation is a formula that can be applied to almost anything. The demonstrative pronouns "this" and "that" stand for variables. We might just as well say, "When there is X, there is Y." And indeed this is basically what the early texts go on to do. They state the formula with different words taking the place of the variables, yielding chains of related statements. These chains have been misinterpreted by modern readers to be linear causal sequences or "chains of events," but the whole point of the doctrine is that multiple factors co-arise in each moment while mutually conditioning one another. The Pali name of this doctrine, *paticca samuppada*, refers to phenomena that come (√*pad*) up (-*ut-*) together (*sam-*) while going (√*i*) back (*pati-*) or depending upon one another. One image used in the text is of sheaves of reeds leaning against each other in a pile—every one falls back upon, depends upon, or "is conditioned by" the others.

No doubt such a universal formula for understanding relationships can be applied to almost any field of inquiry including natural systems, social inter-actions, political dynamics, and historical events. The matter of most imme-diate concern for the Buddha, however, was the field of human experiential phenomenology. He put the doctrine of interdependent origination to work to understand and transform his understanding of four major themes: mind and body, the self, suffering, and liberation. Let's review these briefly.

In every age and culture humans tend to have a general idea of their mind and body as being animated by a sacred spirit or consisting of an underly-ing stable essence. Using meditation to investigate the phenomena of mind and body both carefully and directly, the Buddha instead saw a complex interdependent arising of five related factors or aggregates: material form, feeling, perception, formations, and consciousness. These arise and cease in a continuous swirl of activity, but this activity follows discernable pat-terns of interrelationship. Sit long enough in mindful awareness, and you cannot help but notice this too. One of the first great insights of the Buddha is that impermanence is so thorough that it permeates the mind and body entirely. There is no underlying essence; all psychological and physical fac-tors are arising and ceasing interdependently.

There is, however, in the midst of all this change a discernable *sense* of self. Some unique structures seem to form within experience, some patterns of attitude and behavior are observed to recur, and one does appear able to transform in various wholesome and unwholesome ways. Bringing the for-mula of interdependent origination to bear on this, what is too crudely taken as an agent underlying experience is seen instead as a complex interdependent arising of formations involving intentions, activities of body, speech, and mind, and bundles of dispositions that are laid down over time. As decisions are made, intentions manifest in action, and corresponding dispositions ensue. Change the intentions, and the dispositions will change; when different dispositions exist, different decisions are made. The self is a malleable construct, like everything else, and can be best understood as functioning without essence: self is self-less.

On the night of his awakening the Buddha applied the formula to address the question, "What is the cause of suffering?" The pathology of the human condition too can be mapped out as a complex interdependent arising involving ignorance, craving, grasping, and the view of oneself as a self who suffers. All these factors arise and cease together in patterns of inter-relationship that can be seen and understood. "When there is ignorance, there is desire; when there is desire, there is grasping; when there is grasping, there is becoming a self; when there is becoming a self, there is suffering." These are all factors that "come up together in mutual dependence." In understanding this network of relationships, the Buddha discovered the second noble truth, the origin of suffering.

The solution to the problem of suffering is also discovered using the formula. It turns out there is an interdependent relationship between the psychophysical organism on the one hand and suffering on the other. When ignorance informs decision-making, or craving manifests in experience as a grasping attitude toward feelings, then suffering arises; but when these factors do not arise, then neither does suffering. Consciousness along with its affiliated aggregates will always arise and cease, but whether these are bound up with suffering each moment or not depends upon certain specific relationships. If there is no craving, then feeling arises and passes away without suffering. If there is no ignorance, then decisions are made without accumulating unwholesome dispositions. If there is no regarding of phenomena as "mine," then the self who suffers from attachment to phenomena is not constructed.

Any of these changes will result in the liberation of the mind from suffering, in the extinguishing of the fires of greed, hatred, and delusion, in awakening to buddhahood in this very life. Liberation itself can be understood as a change in the dynamics of the interdependent construction of experience, of purifying the inner landscape of unwholesome states so they no longer encumber and limit the processes of the mind. We get to this point by following the trail of this unassuming formula of causation as it is applied by the Buddha to the phenomenology of moment-to-moment experience.

This knowledge is indeed empowering.

BEYOND PROLIFERATION:
PAPAÑCA

People delight in proliferation,
the Tathagata, in non-proliferation.[36]

Papañca is one of those delightful Pali words that rolls off the tongue (or
bursts through the lips, in this case) and hits the nail on the head. It points
to something so immediate, so pervasive, and so insidious it deserves to
join the English language and enter into common usage. The exact deri-
vation of *papañca* is not entirely clear, but its sense hovers somewhere
between the three nodes of (1) to spread out or proliferate; (2) an illusion
or an obsession; and (3) an obstacle or impediment. The place where these
three meanings converge in experience is not hard to locate. Sit down
with your back straight and your legs folded around your ankles, close
your eyes, and attend carefully to your experience. What do you see?
Papañca.

The term is used to describe the tendency of the mind to (1) spread out
from and elaborate upon any sense object that arises in experience, smoth-
ering it with wave after wave of mental proliferation, (2) which is quite
often illusory, repetitive, and even obsessive, and (3) which effectively
blocks any sort of mental calm or clarity of mind. These are the narrative
loops that play over and over in the mind, the trains of thought pulling out
of the station one after another and taking us for a long ride down the track
before we even know we're aboard. Preeminent Pali translator and scholar
Bhikkhu Bodhi, eloquent as always, calls *papañca* "the propensity of the
worldling's imagination to erupt in an effusion of mental commentary that
obscures the bare data of cognition."[37] Is this starting to sound familiar?

Vipassana meditation has to do with looking deeply into the mind and body to discern the various processes unfolding each moment that fabricate the virtual world of our experience. The riot of conceptual proliferation is often the first thing seen because it is the shallowest and busiest part of the mind. For most of us the monkey mind chatters incessantly as it swings from one branch to another, seizing first this thought, then that idea, then a host of miscellaneous associations, memories, and fantasies. The basic themes around which all this activity swirls, according to the insights of the Buddha, are craving, conceit, and views. We could watch this show all day and learn very little.

As the mind gradually steadies, however, upon the breath or some other primary object of attention, it gains some strength and becomes more calm. Then it is better able to see the stream of consciousness for what it is: a sequence of mind states unfolding one after another in rapid succession. As the foundations upon which mindfulness are established become more stable, one can look upon the flow of experience rushing by instead of being swept away by it. At this point we can begin to explore the inner landscape and, guided by the teachings of the Buddha, discover how things come to be as they are in our little world.

Mind, it turns out, is layered, nuanced, and deep. Working backward from the surface toward its depths, we first notice that papañca, the perambulations of mental proliferation, are based upon thoughts. As the appealingly named *Honeyball Discourse* puts it, "What one thinks about, that one mentally proliferates."[38] Mental proliferation is simply thinking run amok. While it is not necessarily a problem to think (though of course "right thought" is preferable to "wrong thought"), once we get to the level of mental proliferation we are seriously off course and nothing good can come of it.

Looking more closely, we can further discern that thinking is itself based upon perception. "What one perceives, that one thinks about," says the *Honeyball*. Perception is the mental function that makes sense of *what* we are seeing, hearing, smelling, tasting, touching, or thinking. It provides cognitive information about the objects of experience in the form of images, words, or symbols, which are learned in culturally specific ways. We see our world through, as, and by way of perceptions, and more often than not project them onto the world.

Way down under all these layers of mind is a simple moment of contact, the simultaneous coming together of a sense organ, a sense object, and a moment of consciousness that cognizes one by means of the other. This basic awareness is merely an episode of knowing, carrying no content or qualities of its own. All the color and texture of experience, so to speak, is provided by the other concomitant mental factors such as feeling, perception, and the endless permutations of volitional formations. Awareness itself, if we can reach it under all the whirl and spin, is tranquil, luminous, and unadorned.

As the mind moves through the stages of assembling experience, from awareness to perception to conception to proliferation, it moves farther and farther into the realm of macro-construction. At each step we see less of things *as they are* and more of things *as we construe them to be*. Meditation practice works to reverse this process. In the phrases used in the early texts, one abandons obsessive perceptions and thoughts, cuts through mental proliferation, and rests at ease in non-proliferation. And it might not surprise us to hear that those who overcome papañca cross beyond grief and sorrow.

However busy it looks on the surface, the mind at heart is tranquil, luminous, and clear.

DISGUSTED
WITH DHARMA?

S O THERE YOU ARE, happily reading the primary texts of early
Buddhism in order to better understand the essential teachings of the
Buddha. You get to the part that talks about a person practicing in
accordance with the Dharma, knowing things directly as they really are,
and seeing what is impermanent as impermanent with right view. Your head
is nodding in affirmation, "Yeah, that's me all right." Then all of a sudden
you get to the next sentence: "Therefore, one should abide in the *utter disgust* for the aggregates."[39]

"Whoa! Wait a minute . . . What's up with that?" You think there must be
something wrong here. How can the intimate awareness of moment-to-
moment phenomena, the opening to states just as they are, lead to such a
yucky response? We all know the monks and nuns are encouraged to con-
template death, the disintegration of the body in cemeteries, and other
such, well, monastic things; but surely a lay Buddhist vipassana practitioner
(for example) deserves a more positive outlook on life from all this mindful, conscious awareness.

"It's probably just one of those archaic translations," you think, and look
up the passage in another, more modern, translation. But there it is again:
"When a bhikkhu is practicing in accordance with the Dharma, he should
dwell engrossed in *revulsion* toward the aggregates."[40] Checking a third translation yields the term "disregards."[41] That's better, at least, and perhaps offers
a glimmer of how the term might be pointing to something more profound
than merely an aversive reaction. And yet another translation finally points

you in a whole new direction: "When one sees it thus as it actually is with proper wisdom, one become disenchanted with the aggregates."[42]

"What *is* this word, anyway?" you wonder. A little rummaging around in the footnotes and glossaries yields the information that the word being translated as "utter disgust" and "revulsion" is the Pali word *nibbida*. Consulting your handy Pali/English dictionary, you learn that the word is derived from the prefix *nis-* ("without") and the verbal root √*vind* ("to find"), and so most literally means something like "without finding." How do we get from "without finding" to "disgust"?

There is a story in the texts that usefully illustrates the meaning of this most important of terms.

A dog stumbles across a bone that has been exposed to the elements for many months, and is therefore bleached of any residual flesh or marrow. The dog gnaws on it for some time before he finally determines that he is "not finding" any satisfaction in the bone, and he thus turns away from it in disgust. It is not that the bone is intrinsically disgusting; it is rather the case that the dog's raging desire for meat just will not be satisfied by the bone. He is "enchanted" by the prospect of gratification as he scrapes away furiously at the bone, but when he finally wakes up to the truth that the bone is empty of anything that will offer him satisfaction, he becomes disenchanted and spits it out.

The Buddha uses this word at the high end of his teaching. It is not that the novice meditator should practice by regarding things as disgusting. It is not even that an advanced meditator will thereby become disenchanted with the home life and get herself to a nunnery. But the Buddha is suggesting a thorough investigation of all aspects of one's experience, the sort of examination that can only be accomplished by intensive insight over an extended period of time, will eventually yield a deep understanding of the unsatisfactory nature of the conditioned world of constructed experience.

Such an insight, like all Buddhist insights, is not so much a statement about the nature of the world "out there" as it is about the nature of our construction of a world "in here." As I understand the basic teachings of the Buddhist tradition, what is "really out there" is largely irrelevant—partly because we cannot accurately know it, partly because speculating about it pulls us off course, and partly because there is plenty to deal with once the sense data has entered into subjective view by coming into contact with sensory and mental phenomena. The objects of experience are simply "such as they are"; it is the primal need to appropriate these objects for our own (quite literally) selfish purposes that is getting healed by this penetrating wisdom.

The general teaching about turning away from the "external" world, or about finally realizing that one will perpetually "not find" the nutrients we seek in the bleached bones of sensory objects, or about waking from the enchantment cast upon us by a primordial delusion, is not unique to the early Buddhist tradition. The same thought seems to be conveyed in that consummate Mahayana and Zen text, the *Lankavatara Sutra*. In the introduction to his translation of this text D.T. Suzuki brings special attention to what he calls an important psychological event of "turning back" from the world: "technically, it is a spiritual change or transformation which takes place in the mind, especially suddenly, and I have called it 'revulsion.'"[43]

The moral of the story is that it is worth investigating the language one encounters in Buddhist texts—especially the meaning of key technical words. The understanding one gets of *nibbida* lying on the near side of such investigation—turning away in utter disgust from the revolting world—is very different from the meaning that lies on the far side: deeply understanding the conditioned nature of constructed experience, thereby allowing a stance of non-attachment to all phenomena.

SECTION 6
SELF AND NON-SELF

APPEARANCE
AND REALITY

THERE OCCURS A MOMENT in every child's development when she begins to learn that objects do not disappear from existence when no longer in view. By playing peek-a-boo she learns object constancy, which psychologists agree is an essential stage of healthy development. Since the mind can only work directly with "that which appears" in experience, it has to build up a perceptual model of "that which exists" behind or beyond the appearances. This is, of course, just a conceptual construction, but one of such usefulness that it stays with us throughout our lives.

One of the radical aspects of Buddhist meditation is that it invites us to suspend the habit of reflexively ascribing existence to everything experienced, and return to the perceptual simplicity of a phenomenological view. When we attend merely to what appears, as the famous teaching to Bahiya puts it, then "In the seen there will be just the seen, in the heard just the heard, in the felt just the felt, and in the thought, just the thought."[44] As even a passing encounter with meditation will demonstrate, it does not take long in this mode for the reality of the external world to dissolve into irrelevance amid a swirling sea of changing phenomena. The appearances are so apparently real, insofar as they arise and pass away with such astonishing immediacy, that the question of whether or not they are "really real" becomes a mere conceptual curiosity, more distracting than meaningful.

This is an extraordinary feature of classical Buddhist thought. It has never been properly understood, nor can it ever be accepted, by those who share what we might call "the ontological assumption"—that there is something real behind the appearances, more primary and important somehow than the appearances themselves. Nowhere is this assumption more interestingly applied than in the matter of consciousness.

When we hear the word consciousness in English, we immediately speculate that there is a person to whom it belongs, an agent who wields it, or a self that consists of it. Yet early Buddhist texts speak of consciousness only as a process unfolding when certain conditions are met: "In dependence on an organ and an object there arises consciousness."[45] Or, more specifically, "When internally the eye is intact and external forms come into its range, and a corresponding conjunction occurs, then the manifestation of a corresponding instance of consciousness occurs."[46]

The role of consciousness is to serve up an appearance, either from the incoming data of the sense doors or from internal channels of memory, imagination, or conception. Backing this appearance up with a constructed sense of reality is a flourish added by perception. Consciousness is merely an event—the awareness of an object—while perception is the fabrication of an accompanying image or interpretive marker. Both are impersonal activities that occur naturally under certain conditions, and both the agent behind consciousness and the reality behind appearances are convenient but illusory concoctions of the mind.

Why is it, then, that there seems to be such an investment in the reality of consciousness? In Hindu terms the reality (*sat*) and the consciousness (*cit*) of Brahman are inextricable from one another; in Judeo-Christian thought the ultimate creator and sustainer of the entire cosmos is a Person; and even in some forms of later Buddhism it looks as if the finger is pointing to the true self behind the apparent self. Unlike any of these, the Buddha seems to have put forward the remarkable idea that consciousness is merely a set of appearances, as empty of essence as a bubble of foam.

The matter of ultimate concern is not *what* consciousness really *is*, but rather *how* it is manifesting. What is the quality of the experience? With what conditioning mental and emotional factors is consciousness arising in this very moment? The self is something *enacted*, with a supporting role played by consciousness, but with equally important parts provided by the other four aggregates: body, feeling, perception, and formations. Consciousness is shaped by the senses and their corresponding objects, colored by pleasure and pain, textured by the symbolic expressions of perception, and guided by what has been learned in the past, by what is chosen in the present, and by what is acted out in the future. It may all be a show, but its value lies entirely in how well it is performed.

Many say that all religions are ultimately the same, insofar as they are all seeking to discover the true reality behind false appearances. But what if the Buddha was pointing out a very different way of looking at things, one that challenged the most fundamental of all assumptions? His extraordinary insight was that appearances, properly understood as impermanent, interdependent, and unsatisfying, are also devoid of the ontological underpinnings we are used to ascribing to everything in our world. All of it, without exception, is empty—utterly devoid of self.

This may sound like a great loss conceptually, but in experience it is not such a big deal. We are merely suspending a set of habitual perceptual overlays while regarding the phenomena at hand as they are actually presenting in consciousness. "One abides, ardent, mindful, and clearly conscious, observing body as body, feeling as feeling, mind as mind, and mental objects as mental objects," as the classical meditation text puts it.[47] When attending very closely to what appears, the issue of what exists does not even come up. I think the Buddha is telling us we are ultimately better off grounded in the experiential actuality of phenomena than in maintaining the conceptual framework of its alleged reality.

To the young child in her crib, it is reassuring to know her mother does not disappear when her eyes are covered. But when she loses her to old age, sickness, and death, as she surely will some day, it can be even more valuable to learn that her own well-being need not depend on her mother's continuing physical existence. It is the experience that is comforting, and the quality of a mother's love for a child can be enacted at any time by covering the eyes and filling the heart with loving kindness.

KEEPING
YOUR BALANCE

Looking after oneself, one looks after others.
Looking after others, one looks after oneself.[48]

Once in ancient India an acrobat set up his bamboo pole in the center of a village, climbed up the pole with great agility, and balanced carefully upon its tip. He then invited his young assistant to scamper up and stand on his shoulders, saying to her: "You look after my balance, my dear, and I'll look after your balance. With us thus looking after one another and protecting one another, we'll show off our craft, receive some payment, and safely climb down the bamboo pole." "No, no, Master; that will never do!" said the girl. "You must look after your own balance, and I will look after my balance. With each of us thus looking after ourselves and protecting ourselves, we'll show off our craft, receive some payment, and safely climb down the bamboo pole."

The Buddha tells this story in the *Satipatthana Samyutta* to illustrate the practice of mindfulness meditation, and the image of this perilous balancing act works on many levels to help understand what he was pointing to. The physical sense of balance is so immediate, so intimate, and so accessible in every moment of experience it is often the first thing one gets in touch with when sitting down to meditate, and the story derives much of its strength from this fact. We are so used to projecting our attention out into the world around us, it is a noticeable shift when we face inward and feel the subtle swaying of the head on the shoulders, along with all the muscular microcompensations keeping our body centered in gravity. The acrobat, like the meditator, is bringing conscious awareness to a process that is always occurring but is generally overlooked, which is a vital first step to learning anything valuable about ourselves.

The story also vividly demonstrates why it is so important to attend to the quality of one's own inner life before critiquing what others are doing. It's just not possible to keep someone else's balance, and it takes this graphic image to drive home such an obvious truth. Moreover, the acrobat's assistant will only be able to maintain her own balance if the acrobat, upon whose shoulders she stands, is steady and reliable. In other words, the best way he can protect her from harm is to look inward and attend carefully to his own equilibrium. This is true of many things in life.

It describes, for example, the impact a parent has on a child. As we all know, a parent can go on and on about what a child should or should not do, or say, or think, but nothing is going to influence a child's developing personality more than the example actually set by the parent. Not until the mother and father keep their own emotional and moral balance will the child be able to learn how to steady herself upon their shoulders and understand their admonitions. The same applies to the doctor and patient, the teacher and student, the therapist and client, the politician and constituent, the author and reader—indeed to virtually every one of the relationships we form in our world. The quality of every relationship is enhanced by the care brought to it by each party, and this is especially important when one person depends directly upon and trusts the attentiveness of another.

Life itself is a balancing act. We are each of us perched upon a precarious pole, trying to stay centered in a swaying, breezy world. It is difficult enough staying safe ourselves, let alone trying to keep track of all the things stacked upon our shoulders. Mindfulness is a tool for looking inward, adjusting our balance, and staying focused on that still center point upon which everything else is poised. The quality of the present moment of awareness—that bamboo pole upon which we all are perched—can be calm, stable, and focused, and when it is our well-being and that of all those who depend upon us is well protected. When it is not, no amount of pointing to the doings of others can compensate or restore our balance.

One might misconstrue this teaching as selfish. But doing so would involve overlooking the subtle interdependence of self and other the

Buddha goes on to emphasize. The acrobat's attention to his own equilibrium is motivated by his tender regard for the well-being of his beloved
assistant. His initial suggestion that he will look after her balance is an
expression of compassion, but it is not matched by an equal measure of
wisdom. Just as a person mired in quicksand cannot help another until he
has himself reached firm ground (to cite another analogy from the Pali
texts) or, as the flight attendants tell us each time we board a plane, one
must don one's own oxygen mask before helping others do so, our ability
to help others depends chiefly on keeping our own balance.

> Looking after oneself, one looks after others.
> Looking after others, one looks after oneself.
> How does one look after others by looking after oneself?
> By practicing mindfulness, developing it, and making it grow.
> How does one look after oneself by looking after others?
> By patience, non-harming, loving kindness, and caring.[49]

Notice how the boundaries between self and other disappear. By showing kindness and taking care of others, one is being kind to oneself and is caring for oneself. Actually, helping others is the best way to attend to one's
own most basic welfare, just as harming others will invariably harm one's
self or put oneself at risk. According to Buddhist thought, this is because all
action, all *karma*, based as it is upon intention, affects not only the world
"out there" but also one's own dispositions and character. Everything we say
and do and think shapes who we are, just as we go on to shape, through the
quality of our awareness and the depth of our understanding, everything
else in our world. In fact, as I understand this text, it may not be particularly
useful—or even possible—to say where one leaves off and the other begins.

So what is the very best way to protect your child, care for your partner,
contribute to your community, and express compassion for all the world?
Look inward, carefully and often, and keep your balance.

A lot depends upon it.

SELF
IS A VERB

THE CORE INSIGHT of the Buddhist tradition—the relentless emptiness of phenomena—has profound implications for all of us who are trying to understand the nature of life. It points to the disturbing fact that all nouns are arbitrary constructions. A person, place, or thing is just an idea invented to freeze the fluid flow of the world into objects that can be labeled and manipulated by adroit but shallow modes of mind. Beyond and behind these snapshots we take for ourselves is a vast and unnamable process.

Of all the nouns we use to disguise the hollowness of the human condition, none is more influential than "myself." It consists of a collage of still images—name, gender, nationality, profession, enthusiasms, relationships—which are renovated from time to time, but otherwise are each a relic from one particular experience or another. The defining teaching of the Buddhist tradition, that of non-self, is merely pointing out the limitations of this reflexive view we hold of ourselves. It's not that the self does not exist, but that it is as cobbled together and transient as everything else.

The practice of meditation invites us to investigate the flux of arising and passing events. When we get the hang of it, we can begin to see how each artifact of the mind is raised and lowered to view, like so many flashcards. But we can also glimpse, once in a while, the sleight-of-hand shuffling the cards and pulling them off the deck. Behind the objects lies a process. Self is a process. Self is a verb.

So, how do we go about *selfing*? This is something the Buddha looked at very closely, and he left us a trail to follow that reveals the process. The name of this trail is dependent origination, and it starts (in some formulations) with a moment of consciousness, the cognizing of a sense object with a sense organ. Most other thinkers (both then and now) consider the matter to begin and end here, that consciousness *is* self. Where there is an object, there must be a subject, right? Subject and object define one another.

But at least in the earliest teachings of the Buddhist tradition, all that is granted is that consciousness defines an object. To be aware is to be aware *of* something. But as everyone knows—everyone who has lost themselves for a few precious moments in music or dance or sport or nature—one can be fully aware of objects without the corresponding creation of the subject. Selfing is optional.

When an object is known by means of an organ, a moment of contact is born. This is the elemental unit of experience upon which our world of experience is constructed, and is an event that occurs rather than an entity that exists. Perception and feeling also arise in conjunction with this moment of contact, and the whole arisen bundle is further conditioned by a particular intentional stance or attitude. All this amounts to an elegant, but selfless, arising of interdependent physical and mental phenomena (formally labeled the five aggregates), in response to the presentation of information at a sense door. It functions similarly for a suffering worldling or for an awakened Buddha.

The process of constructing a self begins as an uninformed response to the texture of the ensuing feeling tone. Desire is a state of disequilibrium between what is arising and what one *wants* to be arising. The process is the same whether one wants vanishing pleasure to endure or one wants presenting pain to go away. In either case, desire can only manifest when a *person who* desires is created. The self (as a noun) is created as the (imaginary) subject of desire. This is selfing in action.

The manner in which this is done employs the intermediary function of grasping or clinging, which consists of holding on or pushing away. Prompted by desire, the wanting-of-things-to-be-other-than-they-are, the response of holding on to what I like or pushing away what I don't like gets acted out. The making-of-a-self is the verb, and the view-of-a-self is its residue. The two become interdependent and cyclic, since having a view of self will lead one to act out or create the self, which in turn will result in strengthening the view of self, and so on. The issue is not whether the self really exists or not, but how one will regard phenomena in the moment of experience, as with or without self. Hence the Buddhist teaching of non-self is correcting a particular kind of wrong view, rather than negating the existence of an entity. As the matter is put in the Pali texts:

> When there is a self, there is what belongs to my self;
> When there is what belongs to my self, there is a self.[50]

Or:

> This is the way leading to the origination of self (sakkaya): one regards [all phenomena] thus: "This is mine, this is me, this is my self" . . . This is the way leading to the cessation of self: one regards [all phenomena] thus: "This is not mine, this is not me, this is not my self."[51]

What becomes clear through this analysis of moment-to-moment experience is that grasping is not something done by the self, but rather self is something done by grasping. The self is constructed each moment for the simple purpose of providing the one who likes or doesn't like, holds on to or pushes away, what is unfolding in experience. Just as there is a fundamental interdependence between consciousness and its object, so also is there an interdependence between desire and its subject. But there is no inherent bond between subject and object or between consciousness and desire.

The gift bequeathed to us by the Buddha is the possibility of seeing how consciousness can become liberated from desire, allowing it to cognize objects more intimately without the intermediary epiphenomenon of a subject. When desire is replaced by equanimity, and awareness of all phenomena thus unfolds without reference to self, we gain the freedom to move along with change rather than set ourselves against it.

But don't take the Buddha's word for it. Try locating the grasping reflex in your own experience, the subtle attitude of holding on to or pushing away what suits or vexes "me," and see for yourself what happens when it is replaced at any given moment by equanimity.

Selfing is a habit, and like all habits it can either be strengthened by unconscious repetition or broken by the application of conscious awareness and the will to approach things differently. Rest assured that if you manage not to self for a moment or two, you will not cease to exist.

You will, however, cease to cling, and in doing so, for a moment at least, there will be no one who suffers.

THIS WORLD
IS NOT YOURS

IN A DISCOURSE about the teaching of non-self, the Buddha offers the
following illustration: "Bhikkhus, what do you think? If people carried off
the grass, sticks, branches, and leaves in this Jeta Grove, or burned them,
or did what they liked with them, would you think: 'People are carrying us
off or burning us or doing what they like with us?' 'No, venerable sir. Why
not? Because that is neither our self nor what belongs to our self.'"[52]

As we hear this example today, however, we have to admit that it is no
longer entirely true. If that grass were being burned in the Amazon forest,
for example, or if those sticks were being carried off from the foothills of
the Himalayan mountains, there may well be a great number of people who
would be quite disturbed. Why is that? Because one of the fundamental
axioms of the modern environmental movement is that the entire planet is
the precious possession of us all. The very thing that provides for the
preservation of the world's resources is to extend to every blade of grass the
same care and diligent guardianship that we would bring to bear upon our
most intimate possession. In short, it seems that extending the range of the
self to expand and cover the entire earth is the chosen way to protect it
from harm.

Throughout his many teachings, however, Buddha points out that great
harm and suffering emerges from our tendency to define and then protect
the self. The self is a flawed strategy, born in ignorance, nurtured by craving, and perpetuated by endless moments of grasping in which we pull
toward us what we like to consider part of ourselves and push away what we

don't like. Might it be that by enlarging the self to embrace the world we are setting up the conditions for even greater attachment and suffering?

This is not to say the rainforest should not be protected, but suggests that the attitude one brings to the task makes a big difference. There is a lot of work ahead of us, as we endeavor to rescue the planet from ourselves, and we are likely to be at this work for a very long time. Perhaps we could come at it from the wisdom of the non-self perspective, rather than the passions of the "world is mine" point of view. As the Buddha says elsewhere in the same text, "Whatever is not yours, abandon it; when you have abandoned it, that will lead to your welfare and happiness for a long time."

The Buddha had a penetrating insight into human nature. Among the things he noticed is that while some of our best qualities, such as caring, nurturing, and protecting, are directed to the things we feel we possess or own, it is also the case that our worst tendencies, rooted in greed, hatred, and delusion, also organize around whatever is taken to be "mine" or possessed by "me." It can be a useful point of view in the short term or from a narrow perspective, but in the end the self is the source of more harm than good. History offers a sad parade of examples of things being destroyed precisely because they are valued.

The Buddha offers another perspective: Dependent origination provides a model for understanding the profound interrelationship between all things, but it is a model that does not allow for a self. Nothing belongs to anybody; nobody has any self to protect; we all just co-arise with one another.

If the whole world is my self and someone comes along and burns the forest, it is likely that I will respond with anger, hatred, and an urge for revenge. If on the other hand the same action occurs in the context of an attitude of non-self, one still discerns the causal relationship between the action and the suffering it brings to many others inhabiting the same matrix of cause and effect. I can still put a stop to the activity, hold the perpetrator legally and morally responsible for the act, and put in place various safeguards to prevent it from happening again. Now, however, my response is more likely to be guided by wisdom and compassion, and to be grounded in a larger view.

I think the Buddha would argue that one is a more skillful response than the other.

And considering how much is at stake, we need all the skillfulness we can muster.

NO ESSENCE

This body's like a ball of foam,
And feeling is like a bubble;
Perception is like a mirage,
Formations like a pith-less tree,
And consciousness is just a trick.[53]

Throughout the Buddhist tradition, one finds two apparently contradictory models of human nature. One view holds that human beings are fundamentally flawed and laced with impurities, while Dharma training is a heroic struggle to rise above the unwholesome psychological roots that have been entrenched in the mind for incalculable eons. Awakening, then, is a supremely difficult task, requiring unrelenting effort to go "against the stream," as the Buddha said, of our natural tendencies. The other model takes the view that humans are, in our true nature, intrinsically enlightened and virtuous. From this perspective, practice is a matter of uncovering our original purity. The process is based less on striving than on letting go and gently opening up to our innate goodness.

What are we to make of this discrepancy? My own view is that both are true and neither is true—which is to say, they constitute the horns of a dilemma. But if we look to the Buddha's teachings, especially as we find them in the earliest texts, we find that they show us a middle path through this polarity, as through others. Certainly, greed, hatred, and delusion—the traditional three poisons of Buddhist teaching—are deeply embedded in the human psyche, and many of the behaviors that arise from these unwholesome roots deserve the label "evil" (in Pali, *papa*). The mind is permeated with latent tendencies (*anusaya*), hindrances (*nivarana*), defilements (*kilesa*), fetters (*samyojana*), and toxins (*asava*); as the Buddha taught, only a thorough process of purification will allow consciousness to emerge, like a lotus growing up from the mud and blossoming above the waterline, free of the muck and opening to something beyond the world.[54] But it is also said that the mind is naturally luminescent and only appears otherwise because it is defiled by "visiting" contaminants, a word suggesting the one is more foundational than the other. According to this description, human nature contains three wholesome roots: non-greed, non-hatred, and non-delusion (or, put more positively, generosity, loving kindness, and wisdom). There is no reason to suspect that these wholesome roots run any less deep than the unwholesome ones, and indeed they might even be considerably deeper. The pivotal issue, then, is which set of qualities more accurately represents essential human nature.

But the crux of the Buddha's insight was that there are no essences. That being the case, might it not be that it is the very notion of "essential" or "intrinsic" that is causing mischief here? Might the matter simply be one of skillful means—that sometimes it is helpful to emphasize rising above what is unwholesome and at others it is best to speak of uncovering what is wholesome? Either way, what is surely unskillful is to attach to either view. All talk of essences—whether it be of the depressing mass of afflictions or the alluring shine of natural perfection—strikes me as decidedly contrary to the Buddha's teachings, at least as they are presented in the earliest strata of tradition.

It's true that the literature uses terms like "unconditioned" or "deathless," but nowhere does it say that these describe "original" or "essential" aspects of human nature. During the era in which the *nikayas* (the early collections of the Buddha's discourses) were composed such language was a common feature of the Vedas and Upanishads, and were at the very basis of the Brahmanical tradition. In fact, it is likely that the Buddha's teachings of *anatta* (no-self) and *paticca samuppada* (dependent origination) were arguments against these very notions. But he was equally critical of the idea put forward by others, such as the Ajivikas and to some extent the Jains, that the defilements found naturally in human experience are beyond transformation in this lifetime. The middle path between intrinsic goodness and intrinsic evil is the insight that human nature is the product of inter-dependently arising factors—some wholesome, some unwholesome—which manifest moment after moment in lawful and knowable patterns. With mindfulness these patterns can be revealed, with wisdom they can be understood, and, precisely because they are unessential, with practice they can be transformed.

Numerous passages in the early texts emphasize the defective aspects of our human nature and then point to a path of purification leading out of the difficulties. Just to take one almost at random:

> Tangled within, tangled without,
> Creatures are tangled in tangles.
> And so I ask you, Gotama—
> Who can untangle this tangle?
> Those whose passion and aversion
> And ignorance are cleansed away,
> Arahants with toxins destroyed
> —They have untangled these tangles.[55]

But we find as well many passages underlining the natural capacity of the mind for clarity and wisdom. Among the most familiar of these is the following:

> The mind, monks, is luminous;
> it is defiled by defilements that come upon it;
> The mind, monks, is luminous;
> it is purified of defilements that come upon it.[56]

The usefulness of this literature to the student of Buddhism depends on how carefully it is read and how accurately it is understood. As is the case with all sensory perception, the mind is drawn to mental events that co-arise with a pleasurable feeling tone and shies away from those associated with dis-pleasure. This tends to lead our thoughts and views into areas with which we are already familiar and comfortable, and away from what challenges us or causes discomfort. This tendency contributes to polarization in how we think about human nature.

Attachment to experiences that occur in meditation might do the same. Seeing deeply into the relentless arising of painful psychological "stuff" might nudge us to view human nature as defiled; glimpses of magnificent light and clarity might well convince us of our innate purity. In the former case, unwholesome flaws appear more substantial and intractable than the Buddha seems to have regarded them. In the latter, the luminous qualities of mind might be construed more as sacred realities than as the phenomenological manifestations the Buddha described as the field for meditation and transformation.

I suspect we will be better off attending to the nuances of arising and falling experience, below the level of mental constructs, than rearranging the deckchairs of conceptual theory. Whether human nature is inherently good or intrinsically evil might even be irrelevant. The more important issue is what one is doing with the mind right now.

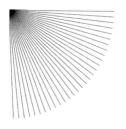

SECTION 7
KARMA

KARMA
IN ACTION

*Beings are owners of their actions, heirs of their actions; they originate from their
actions, are bound to their actions, have their actions as their refuge.*[57]

Karma is a word one runs across more and more these days. It's too bad it is
almost always misused, often as if it means "fate" or "destiny." This is an
unfortunate, if inevitable, distortion, because in its original Buddhist context karma is a concept of unparalleled profundity and significance.

The word karma simply means "action," and is derived from the verbal
root √kr, which means "to do" or "to make." There are three distinct senses
of the word here, and what renders the concept unique is that all three are
inseparable aspects of the same process. We may be used to thinking of (1)
the *decision* to do something as one thing, (2) the *action* carrying it out as
another, and (3) what we *make* thereby, or the result of the action, as being
something else again. But in Buddhist understanding these three are parts
of the same whole. Intention is the leading edge of karma, directing the
activities of body, speech, and mind to act in ways that accumulate, at its
trailing edge, karmic formations or dispositions. Action, in other words, is
preceded by a sort of "doing" in which decisions are made, and results in a
sort of "making" in which a unique personality is constructed. The main
idea behind karma is thus the relationship between what we choose to do
and what we thereby make of ourselves.

This can perhaps best be seen when the word for action is used simultaneously as a verb and a noun, as in the expression *sankharam abhisankharoti*.[58]
There are many ways this can be put into English, such as "one forms formations," "one constructs constructions," "one creates creations," or "one

fabricates fabrications." You get the idea. When action is enacted, so to speak, it involves both the activity of building something and the product of that activity, a building. An image sometimes used to convey this in the texts is of a potter at his wheel. The potter is engaged in the creative process of shaping the clay according to his will, and when the pot is cut off the wheel and fired in a kiln it remains as an enduring artifact of that activity. So also our character, our personality, what we take to be our very *self*, is viewed in Buddhist thought as a gallery of ossified karmic relics, the accumulated residue of earlier dynamic processes of intention and action.

With the outward focus of most Western thinking, we are used to the idea of making choices in response to shifting worldly circumstances, and to the fact that our actions result in changes to our environment. From this perspective, a great emphasis is placed upon what it is we do, and on whether or not our actions are effective in bringing about the external changes we intend. The Buddhist tradition, however, is more interested in the internal dimensions of action. Here the more important questions include "What effect on our own well-being are our decisions having?" and "How are we being changed by our actions?" What we do, from this point of view, is far less important than how we do it. Karma is primarily concerned with how we shape ourselves, and how we are shaped by ourselves, through action.

The self is plastic; it is malleable clay being molded each moment by intention. Just as our scientists are discovering not only how the mind is shaped by the brain but now, too, how the brain is shaped by the mind, so the Buddha described long ago the interdependent process by which intentions are conditioned by dispositions and dispositions in turn are conditioned by intentions. The actions that make up the tangible expression of our lives are merely a go-between, as the world we construct is a mere offshoot of who we are ever *re*-becoming.

In a moment of anger, for example, whether acted out, verbalized, or merely seething unexpressed within, one trains oneself to become angrier by laying down a thin layer (there's the verb and noun again!) of angry disposition. A person so disposed to anger will more and more easily erupt in anger anew at any provocation. But in a moment of kindness a kindly disposition is deposited, and one becomes incrementally more disposed to kindness. The attitude with which we respond to an object of experience, with anger or with kindness, will therefore not only influence the causal field outside ourselves but also progressively reshape our very character.

The secret of who we are is thus found in what we do; yet even what we do is only one phase in a larger cycle of becoming. We inherit our karma from our past, from previous moments of existence in the form of a self—a bundle of dispositions, more precisely—and that past shapes how we understand and construct our present intentions. Yet every moment we also have our future karma in our own hands, as we shape a response to whatever is arising in present experience. This response, which may be more or less wholesome or skillful, is what determines what we will inherit downstream in the flow of consciousness.

The crucial factor influencing how well we can respond in any given situation seems to be the level of mindfulness we can bring to bear upon the moment. If we don't care to be present, unconscious decision-making systems will function by default to get us through to the next moment, albeit in the grips of (often flawed and suffering-causing) learned behaviors and conditioned responses. If, on the other hand, we can increase the amount of conscious awareness present by manifesting mindfulness, we expand the range of our possible responses. Even if disposed to anger, we can choose to act with kindness. This is the essence of our freedom in an otherwise heavily conditioned system.

So karma is not something outside ourselves that happens to us (as we in the West are so used to thinking of everything being), but is something far more intimate and even, although I hesitate to use the word, personal.

WHERE
THE ACTION IS

THERE ARE two aspects to every moment's experience. One is the content, what it is you are aware of; the other is the intention, what your emotional response is toward that object of awareness. In the Buddhist way of looking at things, the first is largely irrelevant, while the second is immensely important.

According to Buddhist psychology, human experience is constructed anew every moment as consciousness of one of the six objects (a form, a sound, a smell, a taste, a touch, or a thought) arises and then passes away. An ongoing sequence of such moments occurs, yielding for each of us a unique subjective stream of experience. We are always aware of something, since consciousness must always take an object—perhaps it is something we are looking at, or hearing, or touching, or thinking.

It is easy to change the content of experience. Close your eyes, and your visual field alters dramatically. Open them, and it all comes rushing back, in impeccable detail. You can choose to remember what you had for lunch last Tuesday, calculate a complex mathematical sum, or fantasize about what you would do if you won the lottery. Our mind/body apparatus is primed for content, and it lurches from one object to another relentlessly and, for the most part, automatically.

The attitude with which all this is done, however, is a different matter. The aggregate called formations (*sankhara*) is so-called because it is constantly forming a response to what is happening. This too is constructed anew each moment. Whenever we are aware of an object through one of the six sense organs, we are simultaneously forming a response to that object. These responses are also part of our unique stream of consciousness, and constitute our emotional life.

When seeing this particular form, we are amused; when hearing that sound, we are annoyed; when smelling this smell, we are disgusted; when feeling that touch, we are aroused; when thinking one thought, we are enraged; when thinking another, we are tranquil. An automaton might merely cognize an object by means of a sense organ; a human being both does this and *responds* with a rich and nuanced emotional range.

The content of experience is largely irrelevant because it is just the data of a perceptual apparatus. Like a camera, the senses—including the mind—can be pointed at just about anything and they will pick up and process information. It does not matter so much what we look at or touch or think, but it matters a lot how we respond to what we are experiencing. This is because all karma is made and passed on by formations. Every emotional response is a form of action, and every action has a consequence. We are shaped not so much by what we do, but by how we *engage* with what we do.

At the heart of the Buddhist path of transformation is the recognition that some responses are healthy, skillful, and propel us a notch closer to being a better person and understanding the nature of things, while others can be quite unhealthy, unskillful, and have the effect of our becoming a slightly more debased person whose delusions only deepen. The emotional responses we enact each moment can be the source of tremendous suffering, both for ourselves and for those around us who are influenced by our actions. The harm comes not from the content, but from the intention accompanying the content of experience. The problem, for instance, is not that I am thinking about someone from another ethnic or social group than my own, it is that I am thinking about that person with hatred, or jealousy, or fear.

The thing is that these intentions we necessarily form in parallel with every moment's awareness of an object are not a mere accompaniment to experience. They go on to condition and determine the actions we will undertake in ensuing experience. One moment's anger becomes the next moment's striking blow, hurtful comment, or nasty thought. We literally build our selves and our world upon our own emotional responses, and indeed it might not be too much to say that who we are and what world we inhabit actually *consists* of the series of these emotional responses unfolding within us.

This puts an interesting face on the idea of practice. Everything is practice, because we are always practicing to be the person we will become next. The reason we put so much time and care and effort into learning, through meditation, how to be with whatever is arising in experience without greed, hatred, or delusion, is because by suspending their influence upon us in this moment, we become free of their effects in the next moment. How we hold ourselves *right now* is the key to everything we will become. It is that important.

So let's focus less upon *what* we are doing, or saying, or thinking, and place greater emphasis on *how* we are doing, saying, or thinking it.

That is where the action is, on the path of transformation.

WHOSE LIFE IS THIS, ANYWAY?

I DON'T KNOW many people in this country who *really* believe in rebirth—do you? I often meet Buddhists of various sorts, and yet it seems that most, like myself, have inherited from their cultural upbringing the "one life to live" model of the human condition. It makes me wonder how much of classical Buddhism we are really capable of absorbing.

When we see how much of who we are now is embedded in our habitual responses to specific conditions in a world we each create from our unique illusions, what could it mean to be "ourselves" in another lifetime? If we have a different body and gender, if our upbringing, language, and learning, our memories, dreams, and attitudes are all different, then how much sense does it still make to call such a person "myself"?

Buddhist doctrine has an answer for this, of course: It doesn't even make sense now for you to call yourself "your self," let alone in "another rebirth." This sense of self is just an assumption from which all our sufferings emerge. The central teaching of Buddhism is to let go of this illusory sense of self, lay down body and mind, cure yourself of the need to believe you are something coherent, independent, or exceptionally meaningful.

I suspect our Western acculturation makes it virtually impossible for any of us to really do this. The notion we have of "ourselves" is just too deeply rooted. Selfhood in the modern West is so intrinsic to our worldview, it is the very water in which we swim or the air through which we fly. "Being" is inconceivable to us without selfhood, as swimming loses meaning entirely without water, or flying without air.

The Buddhist tradition offers up some useful metaphors to help understand rebirth: Like milk changing to curds, then changing to butter and changing again to ghee. Each manifestation is so very unlike each of the others in their particulars, and yet the causal thread connecting them is so evident.

So I am the heir, perhaps, of the deeds of someone long dead. I am grateful to that person, and presumably to many before her, for the karma I have inherited has been fortunate. But I don't relate to that person as having been "me." "I" am somebody that is defined by my body, nationality, language, and by my unique blend of neuroses, all of which are born of and conditioned by the specific context of *this* particular life. I appreciate my former self as an ancestor, but unless I have some direct experience of what it was like to be that person, it is all rather abstract.

We are given the great gifts of life and consciousness, perhaps from an immeasurably long line of beings more or less appropriately called "former selves." We are also given a material world with a delicate ecosystem to support our current needs, and as a special bonus it is populated with a lot of other beings with whom we share it all. And that is about the extent of what we directly experience.

Is this an impoverished picture of the human situation? I think not. Who needs to reach beyond all this wonder surrounding us—consciousness, nature, other beings, a mind and heart that fashion such nuanced constructions? Who needs to feel they will survive their death, either as a transcendent conscious soul residing in heaven or reentering nature again and again? What we are given is precious enough—a moment of awareness. And, if we are fortunate, another, and another.

If it is a sense of gratitude I feel for my forbearer and all her predecessors, it is a great sense of responsibility and benevolence I feel for whatever I will become next: perhaps an astronaut or some other future profession unknown today. Someone will be the heir of my karma—of all my actions, my words, and even the fruits of my thoughts. At the moment of my death I will have spent a lifetime crafting a "self," which I must then hand over to somebody else. And she, too, will take what I have nurtured, will creatively renovate it, and then give it up when her time comes.

The worldview emerging from this perspective on rebirth involves a universe based on *dana*, on generosity. We are the recipients of immeasurable generosity when we are given life, consciousness, a world, and the company of other beings. We are participants in the cycle of giving when we (willingly or not) give up and give back on our deathbed all we have received. The quality with which all this is done is the only thing upon which we have any influence. The quality of each moment of awareness we experience is where our world unfolds, where we construct our character, where our "selves" have any semblance of real existence.

Our lives or our selves can only be said to be "ours" to whatever extent we are aware of them. The last lifetime I was not me but somebody else. Next lifetime I will no longer be me but will have given myself over to another. The same can be said for my past and future in this very life. Was that really me that made that stupid remark years ago? And will it really be the same me that experiences that moment of triumph when I hit the lottery next week? The only part of all this that can be considered in any sense real to me is the present moment, and I lose even this if I am not clearly conscious as it occurs. All the rest is given away.

I think we just have to accept the fact that we will not survive this life. Rebirth in the Buddhist sense, I suspect, has never been about survival. There will be a continuity, and perhaps in many ways the next being can be causally traced back to our actions in this life—but it will be another being, not "me." When the Buddhists say the next being is neither the same nor different from the current being, we tend to hear the part about it not being different (on account of our wishful thinking), and somehow we miss the significance of the part about it also not being the same (on account of our fear of death). A traceable thread of causal continuity from one being to another is a far cry from the sort of personal survival we crave in our bones.

So: How can we help but be bodhisattvas? There is little alternative for us. We are living for the benefit of all beings—whether we like it or not.

The question is only: With what quality will we live this moment?

HOMO SOPHIENS

THE HUMAN SPECIES is evolving, and at a very rapid rate now that the evolution is primarily cultural rather than biological. Physical changes may still occur; but at such a glacial pace we are unlikely to notice anything. Changes in the human mind, however, are dramatic and can be seen all around us.

The twin forces of greed and hatred—the primal urge to want more of what pleases us and to want what displeases us to go away—have been useful adaptive tools throughout our primitive past, but are rapidly becoming obsolete. Now that our communities are global rather than tribal, our tools are powerful rather than rudimentary, and our weapons are capable of massive destruction, we find ourselves in the position of needing to evolve beyond the old paradigms if we are to adapt to the new environment shaped increasingly by our own activities.

The deeply rooted instincts of desire have helped us get to where we are, as they continue to help all animals survive in the wild. Greed is necessary to chase down and devour one's prey, and hatred is essential to the "fight or flight" reflex that helps keep a creature alive in moments of danger. But humans no longer live in small family units in a vast and unfriendly wilderness. Huddled together as we now are, shoulder to shoulder on a shrinking planet, our own animal instincts have become our most dangerous predator.

For whatever reason it happened, the sudden bulging of the forebrain in *Homo sapiens* (which took place not very long ago) gave us humans an unprecedented capability: sustained conscious awareness of what we are doing and how it affects those around us. The Buddhists call this capacity mindfulness (*sati*) and clear comprehension (*sampajana*). It has allowed us to commence the process of evolving beyond the third deeply rooted instinct, delusion, by beginning to develop wisdom.

What is more essentially human than the capacity for wisdom? Wisdom allows us to see beyond appearances into the hidden nature of things; it enables us to perceive what is counter-intuitive; it helps us know what is essential. Wisdom gives us an ability to understand that our greatest happiness and most profound well-being lies beyond the quenching of immediate thirsts or the suppression of unpleasant truths. In particular, wisdom reveals the limitations of our in-born desires of greed and hatred, as it erodes the delusion that holds us in their grip.

The Buddhist tradition can be tremendously helpful to us in the process of trying to evolve to the next level of humanity. The Buddha himself can be viewed as demonstrating what this new species that we might call *Homo sophiens*, "wise humans," might look like. For forty-five years, between the awakening of his mind and the passing away of his body, the Buddha lived with body and mind purified of all states rooted in greed, hatred, and delusion. These three fires had "gone out," had "been extinguished," or had "been released from their fuel," and this is what the word *nirvana* refers to. It describes not a transcendent realm, but a transformed—we might even say evolved—human being.

The goal of becoming a better person is within the reach of us all, at every moment. The tool for emerging from the primitive yoke of conditioned responses to the tangible freedom of the conscious life lies just behind our brow. We need only invoke the power of mindful awareness in any action of body, speech, or mind to elevate that action from the unconscious reflex of a trained creature to the awakened choice of a human being who is guided to a higher life by wisdom.

We do not have to accomplish this in as dramatic a way as the Buddha did. We may not "complete" the work in this lifetime and root out the very mechanism by which our minds and bodies manifest their hereditary karmic toxins. Yet to whatever extent we can notice them as they arise, understand them for what they are, and gently abandon our grasp of them—if for only this moment—we are gaining ground in the grand scheme of things. And even a modest moment of emancipation from the unwholesome roots of greed, hatred, and delusion is a moment without suffering.

Despite the sometimes overwhelming evidence to the contrary, I believe an objective study of history will show that the human species is indeed evolving toward a wiser, kinder, and more noble future. The Buddha and his teachings have had a lot to do with raising the sights of humanity, and we may well be in a position today where these teachings can contribute to a new awakening of human potential.

There is something beautiful in us, eager to unfold. Organic, like a plant, it need only be cleared of choking weeds, watered by kindness and generosity, and turned to the bright, nurturing rays of wisdom.

Mindfulness is the way we can care for this hope; let's claim our freedom and see what we might become.

SECTION 8
THE EMERGENCE
OF MINDFULNESS

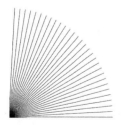

AN ABHIDHAMMA PERSPECTIVE

*The one who fully develops
And fulfills mindfulness of breath,
Practicing systematically
What has been taught by the Buddha,
—He illuminates this whole world,
Like the moon released from a cloud.*[59]

The English language is rich in many ways, particularly when explaining the features of the material world, but it is remarkably clumsy when it comes to articulating the nuanced terrain of inner experience. This is one of the reasons the current conversations about consciousness, meditation, and psychology in general can at times become rather confusing.

One of the satisfactions of studying the languages and literatures of India is the exposure it offers to a richer and more precise vocabulary for speaking about states of mind. At the time Greek philosophers were seeking to identify the universal substances out of which all matter is constructed, their counterparts in India were exploring, empirically and directly, the textures of consciousness. By the time Socrates suggested that care of the soul was an appropriate thing for philosophers to attend to, a detailed and highly developed map of the mind and body as a system of lived experience had been delineated by the Buddha and his immediate followers.

Part of the literature containing this lore is the Abhidhamma. It is an attempt to extract some of the Buddha's core teachings about the phenomenology of experience from the narrative context of the Dharma and to organize it into a more systematic and consistent presentation. I'd like to offer a taste of this greater precision by considering the question, What is mindfulness? As the term grows in importance in contemporary discourse, its meaning seems to be becoming less rather than more clear. Fortunately, the rich vocabulary and meditative insight of the Abhidhamma tradition can help us understand better what the word "mindfulness" is referring to. In the process, this excursion will also include some general observations about how the mind functions, will describe how these functions are augmented by the deliberate practice of meditation, and will address the relationship between the cultivation of mindfulness and the emergence of wisdom.

THE NATURE OF CONSCIOUSNESS

According to the Abhidhamma, consciousness arises and passes away each moment as a series of episodes in a continuing process. It is not a *thing* that exists, but an *event* that occurs—again and again—to yield the subjective experience of a stream of consciousness.

Consciousness itself is rather simple and austere, consisting merely of the cognizing of a sense object by means of a sense organ. This event serves as a sort of seed around which a number of other mental factors crystallize to help consciousness create meaning from the stimuli presenting themselves so rapidly and relentlessly at the doors of the senses.

Like a king with his entourage, as the classical image has it, consciousness never arises alone. It is always attended by a number of other mental factors that help structure, shape, and direct rudimentary consciousness in various ways. The idiosyncrasies of our experience come from the unique configurations formed by all these supporting mental factors as they interact each moment with the changing data of the senses and the synthetic constructions of the mind. Altogether fifty-two of these mental factors are enumerated in the Pali Abhidhamma. (The Sanskrit Abhidharma tradition has a somewhat different list, but we will not get in to that here.) Scholars have tended to dismiss this exhaustive catalogue of mental states as the product of scholasticism run amok, but many people with a mature practice of vipassana meditation are thrilled by the precision with which this literature describes the interior landscape. It is the child of two parents: its mother is deep empirical observation of meditative experience, while its father is an inspired organizing intellect.

Let's go through the Abhidhamma perspective on mindfulness, and you judge for yourself if it is useful or not to your practice. I will identify each mental factor by its Pali term and its number on the list for the sake of clarity, but will not consider all the mental factors nor treat them in their strict canonical order.

UNIVERSAL MENTAL FACTORS

Meditation starts with getting in touch with experience at the point of its inception. We literally make contact (*phasso*, 1) with what is happening in the present moment. If we are daydreaming or worrying or wondering what to do next, we let go of that for the moment and get grounded at one of the sense doors. What is the actual physical sensation arising this moment at the body door as I begin to draw an in-breath? Can I get right to the cutting edge of the sound produced by that chirping bird outside the window? Dropping down from the level of "thinking about" something to "getting in touch" with what is actually occurring *right now* is referred to as making contact with the sensation just as it first arrives at one of the sense doors.

We immediately notice that this sensation is always accompanied by a feeling tone (*vedana*, 2) that can be grossly or subtly pleasant or unpleasant. This is a strand of experience that brings with it a sense of embodiment, an awareness of visceral sensitivity. Every sensation comes with its own distinct quality, with a sense of *what it feels like* to be having that experience right here and now. Even when it is not obviously pleasant or unpleasant, there is nevertheless an affect tone that strings our moments of experience into a continuous flow of feelings, much like the cognitive flow of the stream of consciousness, and contributes to the feeling of being a living organism. Meditation can focus on discerning the distinction between bare sensory contact and the feeling tone that colors the sensation. The stimulus is one thing, while the feeling tone that gives it depth and flavor is another.

Perception (saññā, 3) is another mental factor occurring with every moment of consciousness. Its function is to interpret *what* it is that we are seeing, hearing, smelling, tasting, touching, or thinking in any particular episode of cognition. Perceptions put together knowledge about the presenting object based upon a wide network of associations, memories, analyses, learned perceptual categories, and linguistic labels. These manifest as representations, symbols, words, icons, or other images we might form to interpret the sense data into meaningful categories of thought. This happens automatically and subliminally in every moment, but meditation can bring a heightened attentiveness to the process, so that we become more consciously aware of our perceptions, and the perceptions themselves can become thereby more acute.

So far we have referred to four of the five *khandhas* (in Pali; in Sanskrit, *skandhas*), or aggregates: material form, consciousness, feeling, and perception. Contact is the coming together of the organs and objects of sensation, both materially based, with consciousness, the mental act of knowing one by means of the other. Feeling and perception expand upon this data to fill in a richer picture of what we are experiencing. All four aggregates work together to answer questions like *What is happening here?* and *How am I to understand what is arising in my experience right now?*

Of the fifty-two mental factors listed in the Abhidhamma, two of them (feeling and perception) are aggregates in their own right, while all of the remaining fifty are part of the fifth aggregate, formations (*saṅkhāra*). These address the very different question, *What am I going to do about it?* or *What intentional stance do I take toward this?* Whereas consciousness, feeling, and perception are all based on words built upon the verb "to know," the word for formations is rooted in the verb "to do" and covers the wide range of our emotional responses to what is happening.

The mental factor of intention (*cetanā*, 4) is the active mode of the mind by means of which we exercise our volition or will. Meditation can be understood as an intentional action of paying attention, of being present with, or of otherwise choosing to be aware of what is arising and passing away in the field of experience. Even if one is trying not to direct the mind too much, as in the proverbial "choiceless awareness," there is nevertheless a specific intention to attend carefully to whatever arises. Intention encompasses the executive function of the mind, the faculty by means of which decisions are made and karma is produced. An important nuance of Buddhist thought is that this executive function does not necessarily require an agent exercising it. Choices are made, but there is nobody who makes them—but this is a matter for another forum.

One of the key decisions made by intention is where and how to place one's attention (*manasikaro*, 7), the next mental factor to consider. More than anything, meditation has to do with deliberately directing attention to a particular object of experience. Attending to the breath, attending to an intention of loving kindness toward all beings, attending to the vast sky against which thoughts come and go like clouds—all involve the function of pointing or steering the mind in some non-ordinary way. The definition of daydreaming seems to be allowing attention to wander wherever it will, from one association to another; meditation is a mental discipline wherein the attention is trained to be more selective. Most meditation instructions include such directives as "Allow the attention to settle on . . ." or "Bring attention to bear upon . . ." something or other.

A particular way of doing this is by having attention focus (*ekaggata*, 5) or concentrate upon a single point. This mental factor seems essential to any type of meditation, for by focusing the mind one increases its power significantly. If the mind skips from one object to another in time, or flits from this or that object in space, it can't possibly generate the depth or stability to see anything clearly. One-pointed focus of mind—of consciousness, of intention, or of attention—is a way of harnessing the capacity of the mind to a particular purpose. The Buddhist tradition contains concentration meditations that specifically build upon this function, such as the *jhanas*, or absorptions, but all forms of meditation seem to require some level of focus.

So, are we meditating yet? Remarkably, no.

According to the Abhidhamma, all the above mental factors mentioned are present in every single mind-moment, whether we are meditating or not. All six factors (there is a seventh, but it is not immediately relevant) need to—and automatically do—participate in helping to shape and direct each moment of consciousness. If any one of these factors were absent, we would not be capable of ordinary coherent experience. Even when totally spacing out, or committing a heinous crime, some basic level of contact, feeling, perception, intention, attention, and focus is operative. The presence, and even the cultivation, of these factors alone does not sufficiently account for the practice of meditation.

OCCASIONAL FACTORS

The Abhidhamma next considers a number of factors that are not routinely present in the mind, but may be. When these are absent, we continue to function normally, but when they are present we manifest certain additional capabilities. There are six of these so-called occasional factors, which can arise individually or in various combinations. They are also called ethically neutral factors, because they are not inherently wholesome or unwholesome; they can contribute equally to beautiful or horrific states of mind.

The first of these mental factors is initial application (*vitakko*, 8). This is not a particularly elegant English rendering of the term, but it suits the meaning well enough. It refers to the capability we have to consciously and deliberately place our mind on a chosen object of experience. When you work through a math problem, retell a detailed story, or when you find your mind drifting during meditation practice and (gently, of course) reapply it to the breath, you are exercising this function of applying the mind in a particular way. All discursive thinking is based on this ability to take charge of the mind's attention, so to speak, and is responsible for our prodigious planning and problem-solving skills.

Having directed the mind to a chosen object, another factor is needed to hold it there; this is sustained application (*vicaro*, 9). As you may have noticed, there are considerable forces working to distract your mind and keep its attention moving from one object to another. No doubt this promiscuity of attention has survival value in a rapidly changing environment, but there is also something to be gained by exercising the ability to hold the mind on something long enough to fully understand it and its implications. Concentration meditation, in which one attempts to hold attention steadily on the breath, for example, will be effective only if this focus can be sustained without interruption.

Both initial and sustained application work together to help train and discipline the mind around certain specific practices, such as breath awareness, guided *brahmavihara* practice, and all forms of visualization. Additionally, they may or may not be further supported by energy (*viriyam*, 11). We know what it feels like to do something with or without energy. Sometimes the mind stays easily on course and no particular effort is needed. Other times it is recalcitrant as a mule and needs a firm hand, if not a good kick. Energy is a mental factor that is not naturally always present, and in common idiom we talk about putting forth energy, arousing energy, or otherwise conjuring it up when needed.

Three other factors are considered ethically variable occasionals: decision (*adhimokkho*, 10), joy (*piti*, 12), and impulse (*chando*, 13). Each of these three adds something else to the texture of consciousness, and manifests under different circumstances. Decision, literally in Pali "releasing toward," also means conviction or confidence, and functions when we do or think something with an attitude of decisiveness or determination. Joy is an intense mental pleasure, which can manifest, alas, in either wholesome or unwholesome contexts. And impulse, it is important to note, simply refers to an ethically neutral urge, inclination, or motivation to act, and not to the desire (greed, hatred) rooted in unwholesomeness. If the Buddha eats a meal at the appropriate time, for example, we can say he is prompted to act toward that end without being driven by desire or lust for food. In experience, *chando* can be discerned as the impulse preceding even the most simple and functional actions.

Are we practicing mindfulness yet? We have already seen that if I sit with my legs crossed and back straight, get in touch with the physical sensations of the breath, and intentionally direct my attention to a single point, I am not necessarily meditating. These are all factors that will manifest spontaneously in any endeavor, and are not unique to meditation. If I further apply my mind and sustain its attention on the in-breath, put forth energy with determination, joy, and a self-less inclination for the well-being

of all living creatures, I may well be meditating—but that does not necessarily mean that I am cultivating mindfulness.

MINDFULNESS AND ITS ASSOCIATED STATES

Mindfulness (sati, 29), according to the Abhidhamma, is a wholesome
mental factor that will arise only under special circumstances. In most of the
conventional ways we use the term these days, we are likely to be referring
to any number and combination of the factors already mentioned. In the
classical texts, especially the *Satipatthana Sutta*, one goes to an empty place,
crosses one's legs, straightens one's back and then establishes mindfulness
(sati-upatthana) as an immediate presence. The Abhidhamma offers a four-
fold definition of mindfulness, following the convention of the classical
commentaries: (1) its *characteristic* is not wobbling, or keeping the mind from
floating away from its object; (2) its *function* is absence of confusion, or non-
forgetfulness (the term *sati* comes from a word for memory); (3) its *manifestation* is the state of facing or engaging with an objective phenomenal field;
and (4) its immediate *cause* is strong perception or the four foundations of
mindfulness (i.e., mindfulness of body, feeling, mind, mental objects). These
definitions all suggest an enhanced presence of mind, a heightened attentiveness to objects of experience in the present moment, a special non-
ordinary quality of attention. We can learn a lot more about it by looking
at the company it keeps.

To begin with, it is an axiom of the Abhidhamma system that wholesome and unwholesome mental factors cannot co-arise in the same moment
of consciousness. One can certainly have layers of motivation and a mixed
set of influences coming to bear on any action, but in the precise moment
of initiating an action, says Buddhist psychology, there will be only one
intention dominating the mental process.

Mindfulness is a wholesome factor, so true mindfulness will arise in a
moment of consciousness only if there are no unwholesome factors present.
There are fourteen unwholesome factors, including greed (lobho, 18), hatred
(doso, 21), and delusion (moh, 14) and a number of other afflictive emotional
states deriving from various combinations of these three roots. This means

that if we are feeling envy (*issa*, 22) or avarice (*macchariyam*, 23), for example, these states have our consciousness firmly in grip for the moment; they have hijacked our intention and all the other co-arising mental states, and are directing them to acting and creating karma in an unwholesome way. There can be no mindfulness in such a moment.

The moment immediately following, however, is a whole new beginning. Here we have the option, if we are trained and skillful in the establishment of mindfulness, of taking the envy or avarice that has just passed away as an object of the new moment, with an attitude of mindful investigation. Every moment of consciousness, we might say, has two major components: the object, and the intention with which that object is cognized. A mental object can be almost anything, including unwholesome intentions from previous mind moments; the intention with which it is held here and now will be shaped by the fifty-two mental factors constituting the aggregate of formations (*sankhara*). This means that we cannot be envious and mindful in the same moment, but we can be envious one moment and mindful of that fact the very next moment. Indeed much of what is called spiritual development consists of first becoming aware of what states are arising and passing away in experience (no small challenge in itself), and then of learning how to regard them with mindfulness rather than remaining identified with them or carried away by them (an even more daunting, but not impossible, task).

One of the more astonishing insights of the Abhidhamma is that mindfulness always co-arises with eighteen other wholesome mental factors. We are used to thinking of these factors as very different things, but the fact that they all arise together suggests they can be viewed as facets of the same jewel, as states that mutually define one another. By reviewing the range of wholesome factors that co-arise with it, we can get a much closer look at the phenomenology of mindfulness.

First, there is equanimity (*tatra-majjhattata*, 34). The Abhidhamma actually uses a more technical word for this (literally "there-in-the-middle-ness"), but it is functionally equivalent to equanimity, an evenly hovering attitude toward experience that is neither attracted nor repelled by any object. It is therefore also characterized by non-greed (*alobho*, 32) and non-hatred (*adoso*,

33). This is the generic Abhidhamma way of referring to generosity or non-attachment on the one hand, and loving kindness or friendliness on the other.

You can see how these three work together on a continuum to delineate perhaps the most salient characteristic of mindfulness. When true mindfulness arises, one feels as if one is stepping back and observing what is happening in experience, rather than being embedded in it. This does not mean separation or detachment, but is rather a sense of not being hooked by a desirable object or not pushing away a repugnant object. There in the middle, equidistant from each extreme, one encounters a sense of freedom that allows for greater intimacy with experience. It may seem paradoxical, but this system suggests we can take an attitude toward the objects of experience that is at the same time both equanimous and benevolent. Loving kindness manifests as a deeply friendly intention toward another's well-being, but it is not rooted in any selfish desire for gratification. Similarly, generosity co-arising with equanimity indicates that a deep intention to share something valuable with another can manifest without a desire for reciprocal gain.

Also engaged with all these mental factors are the twin "guardians of the world," self-respect (*hiri*, 30) and respect for others (*ottappam*, 31). I find these translations preferable to the more common "moral shame" and "moral dread," for obvious reasons—such English words carry with them unfortunate baggage that has no place in Buddhist psychology. The first of these constitutes an indwelling conscience, by means of which we know for ourselves whether or not an action we are doing or are going to do is appropriate. The second term is more of a social or interpersonal version of conscience. As mammals I think we have adaptive instincts for empathy toward other members of the group, and reflexively understand whether we are thinking, speaking, or acting within or outside the social norm. These two factors, self respect and respect for others, are called guardians because they are always operative in all wholesome states, while their opposites, lack of self-respect (*ahirikam*, 15) and lack of respect for others (*anottappam*, 16) are present in every single unwholesome state.

Next, we have faith (*saddha*, 28), always co-arising with mindfulness. Every moment of mindfulness is also a moment of confidence or trust; it is not a shaky or tentative state of mind, and is the antithesis of unwholesome doubt (*vicikiccha*, 27). There remains only to consider a group of six associated factors, each with two aspects (therefore numbering twelve, 35–46). These terms can be taken almost as adjectives of mindfulness: tranquility, lightness, malleability, wieldiness, proficiency, and rectitude. Experientially, these qualities can serve as useful indicators to when true mindfulness is manifesting. If you are regarding an object of experience during meditation with any restlessness, for example, or with heaviness, or with rigidity, you can be sure that mindfulness is not present. By the same token, mindfulness is sure to be present when all six of these qualities arise together, each mutually supporting and defining one another. It is all at once a peaceful, buoyant, flexible, effective, capable, and morally upright state of mind.

THE CULTIVATION OF MINDFULNESS

With all that has been said it may seem that mindfulness is a rare occurrence, arising only under the most exotic of conditions. In fact, however, it is quite natural, something we all experience often in one context or another. The cultivation of mindfulness as a meditation practice entails coming to know it when we see it, and learning how to develop it. The Pali word for development is *bhavana*, which simply means "causing to be." The core meditation text *Discourse on the Establishment of Mindfulness (Satipatthana Sutta)* offers simple instructions on how to do this:

> As mindfulness is internally present, one is aware: "Mindfulness is internally present in me." As mindfulness is not internally present, one is aware: "Mindfulness is not internally present in me." As the arising of unarisen mindfulness occurs, one is aware of that. As the arisen mindfulness is developed and brought to fulfillment, one is aware of that.[60]

In mindfulness meditation we work to create the conditions favorable to the arising of mindfulness, relaxing the body and the mind, focusing the attention carefully but gently on a particular aspect of experience, while producing sufficient energy to remain alert without losing a sense of ease and tranquility. Under such conditions, properly sustained, mindfulness will emerge as if by some grace of the natural world, as if it were a gift of clarity from our deepest psyche to the turbid shallows of our mind. When it does, we gradually learn how to hold ourselves so that it lingers, to relocate or reenact it when it fades, and to consistently water its roots and weed its soil so that it can blossom into a lovely and sustainable habit of heart and mind.

As much as the scientific community currently enthralled with mindfulness would like to set aside the ethical component of the Buddhist tradition to focus their studies on the technology of meditation, we can see from this Abhidhamma treatment of the subject that true mindfulness is deeply and inextricably embedded in the notion of wholesomeness. Although the brain science has yet to discover why, this tradition nonetheless declares, based entirely on its phenomenological investigations, that when the mind is engaged in an act of harming it is not capable of mindfulness. There can be heightened attention, concentration, and energy when a sniper takes a bead on his target, for example, but as long as the intention is situated in a context of taking life, it will always be under the sway of hatred, delusion, wrong view (*ditthi*, 19), or some other of the unwholesome factors. Just as a tree removed from the forest is no longer a tree but a piece of lumber, so also the caring attentiveness of mindfulness, extracted from its matrix of wholesome co-arising factors, degenerates into mere attention.

One final question remains to be asked: As we practice the true development of mindfulness, are we also cultivating wisdom? If meditation (*samadhi*) is the bridge between integrity (*sila*) on one hand and wisdom (*pañña*) on the other, does mindfulness lead inevitably to wisdom? The discomforting answer to this question is again, no. The Abhidhamma lists wisdom (*pañña*, 52) as the last of the mental factors. Wisdom is certainly a wholesome factor, but it is not a universal wholesome factor and so does not arise automatically along with mindfulness and the rest.

Wisdom, understood as seeing things as they really are, is the crucial transformative principle in the Buddhist tradition. Just as you can be attentive without meditating and can practice meditation without manifesting mindfulness, so also you can practice mindfulness without cultivating wisdom. If mindfulness is not conjoined with insight (another word for wisdom), it will not in itself bring about a significant change in your understanding. Real transformation comes from uprooting the deeply embedded reflex of projecting ownership upon experience ("this is me, this is mine, this is what I am"), and seeing it instead as an impermanent, impersonal, interdependent arising of phenomena. Cultivating mindfulness is a crucial condition for this to happen, but will not in itself accomplish that end. As one text puts it, mindfulness is like grabbing a sheath of grain in one hand, while wisdom is like cutting it off with a sickle in the other.[61]

As with the arising of mindfulness, so also for the arising of wisdom: it cannot be forced by the will or engineered by the technology of meditation. Yet the conditions which support the emergence of wisdom can be patiently and consistently cultivated, moment after mindful moment, until it unfolds as of its own accord, like the lotus bursting out above the water, or the moon flashing suddenly from behind a cloud.

This is hardly the last word on the subject, but I suspect the foregoing analysis raises the bar somewhat on how we use mindfulness as a technical term. Two things at least seem quite clear: there can scarcely be a more noble capability of the mind than mindfulness, and its cultivation must surely be one of the more beneficial things we can do as human beings.

NOTES

All translations from the Pali are by the author.

1   *Samyutta Nikaya* 22:91
2   *Samyutta Nikaya* 35:93
3   *Cullavagga* 6:4.4
4   *Majjhima Nikaya* 22
5   *Majjhima Nikaya* 38
6   *Anguttara Nikaya* 2:3.3
7   *Anguttara Nikaya* 2:2.10
8   *Digha Nikaya* 16:4.8
9   *Anguttara Nikaya* 3:65
10 *Mahavagga* 8:26
11 *Sigalakovada Sutta, Digha Nikaya* 31
12 *Majjhima Nikaya* 19
13 *Sutta Nipata* 935–39
14 *Samyutta Nikaya* 35:28
15 *Sutta Nipata* 642
16 *Maha Niddesa* 1:42
17 *Samyutta Nikaya* 43
18 *Majjhima Nikaya* 38
19 *Majjhima Nikaya* 146
20 *Majjhima Nikaya* 2
21 *Anguttara Nikaya* 4:45

22   The √ symbol is used to indicated the verbal root from which a term
     derives.

23   *Majjhima Nikaya* 152

24   *Majjhima Nikaya* 131

25   *Anguttara Nikaya* 1:4

26   *Anguttara Nikaya* 5:51

27   *Anguttara Nikaya* 1:4

28   *Samyutta Nikaya* 35:247

29   *Majjhima Nikaya* 19

30   *The Middle Length Discourses of the Buddha: A New Translation of the Majjhima
     Nikaya.* Bhikkhu Nanamoli and Bhikkhu Bodhi, Wisdom Publications,
     1995, p. 193.

31   *Samyutta Nikaya* 11:1.4

32   *Samyutta Nikaya* 11:1.4

33   *Samyutta Nikaya* 12:37

34   *Samyutta Nikaya* 12:37

35   *Mahavagga* 1:23

36   *Dhammapada* 254

37   *The Middle Length Discourses of the Buddha*, n. 229

38   *Majjhima Nikaya* 18

39   *The Book of the Kindred Sayings*, vol iii (*Samyutta Nikaya*). F. L. Woodward,
     Pali Text Society, 1975, p. 36.

40   *The Connected Discourses of the Buddha: A New Translation of the Samyutta
     Nikaya.* Bhikkhu Bodhi, Wisdom Publications, 2000, p. 882.

41   *The Middle Length Sayings.* Translated from the Pali by I. B. Horner, Pali
     Text Society, 1976, p. 231.

42   *The Middle Length Discourses of the Buddha*, p. 279.

43   *The Lankavatara Sutra.* Translated from the Sanskrit by D.T. Suzuki, Pra-
     jna Press, Boulder 1978, p. xvii.

44   *Udana* 1:10

45   *Samyutta Nikaya* 35:93

46   *Majjhima Nikaya* 28

47   *Majjhima Nikaya* 10

48   *Samyutta Nikaya* 47:19

49   *Samyutta Nikaya* 47:19

50   *Majjhima Nikaya* 22

51   *Majjhima Nikaya* 148

52   *The Middle Length Discourses of the Buddha*, p. 235.

53   *Samyutta Nikaya* 22:95

54   *Theragatha* 700–701.

55   *Samyutta Nikaya* 1:13

56   *Anguttara Nikaya* 1:5

57   *Majjhima Nikaya* 135

58   *Samyutta Nikaya* 12:51

59   *Theragatha* 548

60   *Majjhima Nikaya* 10

61   *Milinda Pañho* 2:1.8

ACKNOWLEDGMENTS

MANY PIECES in this volume have been published singly in slightly different forms. I offer grateful acknowledgment to *Insight Journal*, *Buddhadharma*, and *Tricycle* for having printed them originally.

Versions of the following pieces appeared in *Insight Journal*, quarterly journal of the Barre Center for Buddhist Studies: "What the Buddha Taught" (Spring 06); "An Organic Spirituality" (Fall 05); "The Non-Pursuit of Happiness" (Spring 04); "The Post-Copernican Revolution" (Winter 08); "Healing the Wounds of the World" (Fall 02); "War and Peace" (Fall 04); "Making the Best of It" (Summer 07);" Interconnected . . . Or Not?" (Spring 05); "This World Is Not Yours" (Winter 06); "Where the Action Is" (Summer 08); "Whose Life Is This, Anyway?" (Fall 03); "Homo Sophiens" (Spring 03).

Versions of the following pieces appeared in *Buddhadharma: The Practitioner's Quarterly*: "Beyond Proliferation: *Papañca*" (June 06); "Disgusted with Dharma?" (Fall 03); "An Abhidhamma Perspective" (Fall 08).

Versions of the following pieces appeared in *Tricycle: The Buddhist Review*: "Removing the Thorn" (Fall 06); "Burning Alive" (Winter 09); "This Fathom-Long Carcass" (Spring 05); "Unreal Imagination Exists" (Spring 09); "In the Blink of an Eye" (Spring 06); "Tug of War" (Summer 07); "Changing Your Mind" (Winter 06); "Calm in the Face of Anger" (Fall 06); "Caring for Each Other" (Summer 08); "Interdependence" (Spring 07); "Keeping Your Balance" (Summer 06); "Self Is a Verb" (Spring 05); "No Essence" (Winter 05); "Karma in Action" (Fall 08).

INDEX

A
Abhidhamma tradition, 163–75
abuse, 8, 53
adaptation, 29–30
addiction, 6, 8
agency, notion of, 9–10
aggregates, 110, 117–18, 132,
        149–50, 166, 171
Alexander, 25
alienation, 107
altruism, 30, 35
Ananda, 39
anger, 48, 96, 99–102, 150
    karma and, 146–47
    selfhood and, 136
Anumana Sutta, 96–98
archeology, 2
architecture, of the brain, 2, 61
Arittha, 22
Aryan migration, 26
asankhata, 62
asceticism, 25
Ashoka (king), 26

astronomy, 33, 55
attachment. *See also* non-attachment
    awakening and, 15
    as a form of desire, 52
    interdependent origination and,
        13
    warfare and, 49
Attadanda Sutta, 51
attention, dispersion of, 83–85
aversion, 49, 52, 79
awakening, 14–16, 57. *See also*
        enlightenment
    unreal imagination and, 74
    unwholesome states of mind
        and, 95
B
Bahiya, 123
balance, keeping your, 127–29
behaviorism, 1
Bodhi, Bhikku, 113
bodhisattvas, 155
body. *See also* brain; breath; sense
        experience

disintegration of, contempla-
    tion of, 117
interdependent origination and,
    12–14
karma and, 145
keeping your balance and,
    127–29
mindfulness and, 71, 173–75
selfhood and, 153
stress and, 85
Brahmanical tradition, 26, 124, 140
brain, 2, 12, 69, 88
evolution of, 157–58
shaping of, by the mind, 146
two approaches to understand-
    ing, 61–63
breath, 27, 71, 85
Abhidhamma tradition and,
    165, 167
mindfulness of, 89
Buddha, 29, 34–35, 125, 136, 159
Abhidhamma tradition and,
    163–64
awakening and, 14–15, 57
on the battle between gods and
    demons, 99–100
on "burning" emotions, 55, 56
on caring, 39, 40
on consciousness, 65–67
on craving, 15
death of, 63
dependent origination and,
    106, 109, 110, 136
on desire, 52, 78

on a developed mind, 84
the Dharma and, 22–23, 26,
    117–19
on doing one thing at time, 85
on equanimity, 79–80
on the extension of material
    world, into space, 65, 67
on fear, 51–52
Four Noble Truths and, 41
on keeping one's balance, 127,
    129
on happiness, 30, 31, 32
impermanence and, 5
on mental states, 48
purification and, 140, 158
in the *Satipatthana Samyutta*,
    127–29, 170
selfhood and, 131–32, 135
on suffering, 77, 111
teachings of, 21–23
on true security, 43–45
on the "twin guardians" of the
    world, 53
on undisciplined minds, 91–93
on unrestrained minds, 83
on wholesome and unwhole-
    some states of mind, 95

C
cause and effect, 10–14, 61, 79, 95,
    136
change, 4–6, 30–32. *See also*
    impermanence
childhood, 123, 125, 128–29

Christianity, 43, 106, 124

clear comprehension, capacity for, 158

clinging, 11, 75, 132, 134

compassion, 47, 48, 75, 129
  anger and, 102
  healing and, 15–16
  innate impulses toward, 78
  selfhood and, 136

concentration, 84–85, 167, 169

consciousness
  appearances and, 123–25
  the Buddha on, 65–67
  as conditioned, 62, 63
  delusion and, 69–71
  dependent origination and, 12–14
  impermanence and, 5
  karma and, 147
  meditation and, 17
  nature of, 164–65
  as one of the five aggregates, 110–11
  papañca and, 114–15
  purification and, 140
  rebirth and, 154
  six modes of, 87, 88
  stream of, 69
  as a tool for transforming our unconscious, 70–71
  unconditioned, 62
  unreal imagination and, 73–75

Copernicus, 33–35, 65, 95

craving, 8, 13, 15, 78, 114

D

Dalai Lama, 3

death, 22, 47, 63, 117, 154

defilements, 27, 140–42

delusion, 47, 55–57, 69–71, 89, 158
  Abhidhamma tradition and, 174
  absence of, 62
  as embedded in the human psyche, 139
  human nature and, 140
  inner guardians and, 53
  unwholesome states of mind and, 95
  warfare and, 47

dependent origination, 11–14, 105–6, 110, 136, 140

desire, 30–31, 79, 157, 172
  the Buddha on, 52, 78
  selfhood and, 132
  two forms of, 52

Dhammapada, 95

Dharma, 41, 117–19, 139, 163–64
  the Buddha on, 22–23, 26
  dependent origination and, 109
  discipline, 84, 167
  divorce, 44

dukkha. See suffering

dysentery, 39, 40

E

ecology, 12, 29, 135

empathy, 2, 15–16

emptiness, 131

enemy, use of the term, 105
enlightenment, 139. *See also*
    awakening
environmental issues, 12, 29, 135
equanimity, 7, 78, 79
    the Buddha on, 79–80
    selfhood and, 133, 134
essence, notion of, 139–42
ethics, 3–4, 10, 169, 174. *See also*
    morality
evil, 49, 107, 139, 141, 142

F
fear, 45, 48–49, 51, 52
five aggregates, 110, 117–18, 132,
    149–50, 166, 171
formations, 149–50
Four Noble Truths, 6–8, 41, 111
freedom, 17, 79, 159, 172
    anger and, 101
    journey from suffering to, 77–80
    selfhood and, 133
    undisciplined mind and, 91, 92,
    93
Freud, Sigmund, 15

G
Ganges River, 25
generosity, 44, 47, 56, 155, 159
    Abhidhamma tradition and, 172
    innate impulses toward, 78
Great Chain of Being, 106
greed, 55–57, 62, 95, 139, 171
    as an adaptive response from a

    primitive past, 157, 158
    human nature and, 140
    inner guardians and, 53
    interconnectedness and, 107
    warfare and, 47
Greek philosophy, 163
guardians, inner, 53–54

H
hatred, 55–57, 139, 174
    absence of, 62
    as an adaptive response from a
        primitive past, 157, 158
    aversion and, 52
    human nature and, 140
    inner guardians and, 53
    interconnectedness and, 107
    selfhood and, 136
    unwholesome states of mind
        and, 95
    warfare and, 47, 48
hermeneutics, 21
hindrances, 140
Hinduism, 25, 74, 124
hiri, 53–54, 172
honesty, 44, 54
Honeyball Discourse, 114
Huineng, 106
human nature, 2, 136, 140–42
human rights, 1, 56

I
idealism, 34
ignorance, 13, 47

illness, 39, 44, 107. *See also* pain;
    suffering
illusion, 73–75
imagination, 73–75, 124
impermanence, 4–6, 12–13, 63. *See*
    also change
India, 2, 25–26, 127
Indriyabhavana Sutta, 77
Indus River Valley, 2, 25
instinct, 6, 78
integrity, 16–18
interdependence, 4, 43–45, 63,
    109–12
    karma and, 146
    selfhood and, 133
"internonattachedness," coining of
    the term, 107
Islamic tradition, 43

J
Jainism, 25, 140
jhanas, 167
Judaism, 43, 124

K
Kalamas, 23
karma, 40, 49, 129, 154, 158. *See*
    also rebirth
    in action, 145–147
    unwholesome states of mind
        and, 95
    use of the term, 145
Khyber Pass, 26
killing, 48, 56

kindness, 44, 47, 48, 75, 159. *See*
    also compassion
    innate impulses toward, 78
    karma and, 146–47

L
Lankavatara Sutra, 119
letting go, 31, 75, 79, 85, 139
love, 17, 44
loving kindness, 125, 167

M
Madhyantavibhaga, 73
Mahayana tradition, 62, 119
Maitreya, 73
Majjhima Nikaya, 77, 96–98
mantras, 43
Mara, 89
Matali, 99–100
materialism, 66, 106
MBSR (Mindfulness-Based Stress
        Reduction) programs, 8
meditation, 2, 3, 31, 131, 142
    Abhidhamma tradition and,
        165–68, 173–75
    in ancient India, 25
    appearances and, 123
    concentration meditation, 167,
        169
    cultivation of mindfulness
        through, 173–75
    impermanence and, 6
    integrity of consciousness and,
        17–18

interconnection and, 106

papañca and, 114–15

practice, of psychotherapists, 2

prescription of, by the Buddha,
    52–53

the unconscious and, 70

vipassana meditation, 114, 117,
    165

mental factors, 164–73

Middle East, 43

mind

changing your, 95–98

matter and, relationship of, 62

"monkey," 5, 85, 114

the present moment and, 87–89

undisciplined, 91–93

unlimited, 93

unreal imagination and, 74–75

mindfulness, 13, 57, 127–29, 159,
    170–75

Abhidhamma tradition and,
    165–73

anger and, 101

-based stress reduction pro-
    grams, 8

capacity for, 158

collective, 53

insight and, 78–79

integrity and, 16–18

karma and, 147

non-self and, 10

peace and, 85

prescription of, by the Buddha,
    52–53

sense experience and, 92

states associated with, 170–73

monastic community, 39, 40

morality, 136, 172. See also ethics

multitasking, 83

N

neurons, 61, 63, 69

neuroscience, 10, 34, 62

nibbana, 62

nibbida, 118, 119

nihilism, 6

nikayas, 140

nirvana, 14–16, 158. See also
    awakening

non-attachment, 119. See also
    attachment

non-self, 4, 8–9, 12, 131–34, 136.
    See also self

nuclear weapons, 44

O

objectivism, 21, 33, 35, 66

objectivity, 16

objects, 13–14, 16, 88, 149,
    168–70

Abhidhamma tradition and,
    167, 172, 173

concentration on, 84

knowledge of, 66–67

selfhood and, 132, 133

subjectivity and, relationship
    of, 132

occasional factors, 168–70

oil lamp metaphor, 62
ontology, 9, 62, 66, 74, 123–24
organic spirituality, 25–28
otherness, 25, 27, 71
ottappa, 53–54

P
pain, 7–8, 27. *See also* suffering
papañca, 113–115
paradigms, 26, 157
parenting, 44, 128–29
parikalpa, 73, 75
pathology, tendency to focus on, 14
paticca samuppada. *See* dependent origination
peace, 47–49, 52, 85
    awakening and, 15
    sense experience and, 89
perfection, 26, 74, 140
phenomenology, 66, 74, 78, 123
pleasure, 6–8, 13, 93, 77–78, 132
pluralism, 75
process thinking, 106
psychology, 1–3, 123, 149, 172
psychotherapy, 2–3
purification, 140, 158

R
rebirth, 153, 154, 155. *See also* karma
responsibility, 40, 154
revulsion, 117–119
Russia, 44

S
Sakka, 99–101
samadhi. *See* concentration
Samyutta Nikaya, 99
Sati, 22
Satipatthana Samyutta, 127–29, 170
security, source of true, 43–45
self, 5, 27, 153–55. *See also* non-self
    appearances and, 123–25
    the Buddha on, 135
    definition and protection of, harm caused by, 135–36
    enlargement of, 135–36
    interconnectedness and, 107, 110–11
    karma and, 146, 147
    the other and, 71
    plasticity of, 146
    as a verb, 131–34
sense experience, 85, 141, 164, 165
    attending to, training in, 89
    delusion and, 69
    five strands of, 87–89
    happiness and, 30, 31
    mental objects and, 66–67
    mindfulness of, 89
    papañca and, 114–15
    present moment and, 87–89
    suffering and, 77
    undisciplined mind and, 91–93
skillful means, 140
soul, 9, 10, 65–66, 74, 154
Soviet Union, 44
stress, 8, 49, 85

subjectivity, 65
suffering
    the Buddha on, 111
    delusion and, 70
    end of, 77–80
    fact of, as a core insight of
        Buddhism, 4, 6–8
    happiness and, 30
    interconnectedness and, 107
    introspection and, 27
    karma and, 147
    origin of, 111
    selfhood and, 132, 134, 136,
        153
Suzuki, D. T., 119
systems theory, 29

T
Tathagata, 22
terrorism, 45
Theravada tradition, 62
thorn, metaphor of a, 15, 51–54
toxins, 140, 158

U
unconditioned consciousness, 62
unconscious, 2, 47, 61, 70–71, 78
Upanishads, 26, 140
Uttara, 77

V
Vajrayana tradition, 62
Vedic tradition, 26, 140
vegetarianism, 26

Vepacitti, 99–102
verb, the self as a, 131–34
violence, 45, 52
vipassana meditation, 114, 117,
        165
visualization, 169

W
warfare, 45, 47–49
water-jug metaphor, 89

Y
yoga, 25
Yogachara tradition, 73

Z
Zen Buddhism, 106, 119

ABOUT
THE AUTHOR

ANDREW OLENDZKI is a Buddhist scholar, teacher, and writer living in Amherst, Massachusetts. Trained at Lancaster University (UK), the University of Sri Lanka (Perediniya), and Harvard, he was the first executive director at the Insight Meditation Society in Barre, MA, and went on to lead and teach at the Barre Center for Buddhist Studies for twenty-five years. He has also taught at numerous New England colleges (including Amherst, Brandeis, Connecticut, Hampshire, Harvard, Lesley, Montserrat, and Smith colleges), spent two years at the Mind & Life Institute heading up their Mapping the Mind project, and has been a longtime member of the Institute for Meditation and Psychotherapy. Andrew has contributed chapters to many books on Buddhist psychology, writes regularly for *Tricycle: The Buddhist Review*, and is the author of *Untangling Self*. He is currently creating and teaching a number of online courses as the senior scholar of the Integrated Dharma Institute.

PUBLISHER'S ACKNOWLEDGMENT

THE PUBLISHER GRATEFULLY ACKNOWLEDGES the generous help of the Hershey Family Foundation in sponsoring the publication of this book.

WHAT TO READ NEXT
FROM WISDOM PUBLICATIONS

Untangling Self
A Buddhist Investigation of Who We Really Are
Andrew Olendzki

"Brilliant! A breathtakingly clear synthesis of a vast body of early Buddhist teachings."—Christopher Germer, PhD, author of *The Mindful Path to Self-Compassion*

Abhidhamma Studies
Nyanaponika Thera

"One of the most profound and lucid interpreters of Buddhist psychology in our time."—Daniel Goleman, author of *Emotional Intelligence*

Nothing Is Hidden
Barry Magid

"A nuanced, sensitive, and compassionate analysis. This book can help point toward more honest introspection that will yield healing and acceptance."—*Publishers Weekly*

MindScience
His Holiness the Dalai Lama

"A nuanced, sensitive, and compassionate analysis. This book can help point toward more honest introspection that will yield healing and acceptance."—*Publishers Weekly*

About Wisdom Publications

Wisdom Publications is the leading publisher of classic and contemporary Buddhist books and practical works on mindfulness. To learn more about us or to explore our other books, please visit our website at wisdompubs.org or contact us at the address below.

Wisdom Publications
199 Elm Street
Somerville, MA 02144 USA

We are a 501(c)(3) organization, and donations in support of our mission are tax deductible.

Wisdom Publications is affiliated with the Foundation for the Preservation of the Mahayana Tradition (FPMT).